Designing and Using Portfolios

Beverly D. Shaklee
Kent State University

Nancy E. Barbour
Kent State University

Richard Ambrose
Kent State University

Susan J. Hansford
Cleveland Heights–University Heights Schools, Ohio

Allyn and Bacon

Boston   London   Toronto   Sydney   Tokyo   Singapore

Copyright © 1997 by Allyn & Bacon
A Viacom Company
160 Gould Street
Needham Heights, MA 02194

Internet: www.abacon.com
America Online: keyword: College Online

The contents of this book were developed, in part, from a grant from the Department of Education. However, these contents do not neces-sarily represent the policy of the Department of Education and you should not assume endorsement by the Federal Government.

Library of Congress Cataloging-in-Publication Data

Designing and using portfolios / Beverly D. Shaklee ... [et al.].
     p.   cm.
    Includes bibliographical references.
    ISBN 0-205-16259-2
    1. Portfolios in education--United States.   2. Educational tests and measurements--United States.   I. Shaklee, Beverly D.
    LB1029.P67D47   1997
    371.27--dc21   96-39374
                                            CIP

Printed in the United States of America
10 9 8 7 6 5 4 3 2 1   01 00 99 98 97

Contents

Preface

Change does not come easily. In our work with teachers who were committed to applying alternative forms of assessment with students, we discovered how difficult it was for them to develop comfort in letting the traditional forms of assessment go. It was clear to us that teachers need to have confidence about the shift in practice. They need to have concrete examples of how the process of portfolio assessment will account for students' growth and progress.

As a result of our work with the Early Assessment for Exceptional Potential project, a Jacob Javits funded grant, we learned much about what resources were necessary for teachers to truly embrace the portfolio assessment approach. Teachers must have models, structures for decision making, time to learn new management strategies, and collaborative support. Because not every school district or even every individual teacher is able to access the kind of support we had built into the grant, we decided to compile our ideas of how one makes the move to portfolio assessment with or without the ideal collaborative support and professional development opportunities we constructed.

Our book, *Designing and Using Portfolios,* is a straightforward approach to introduce the notion of portfolio assessment to both pre-service and in-service teachers. It explains the portfolio process as a decision-making framework and leads the reader through the actual decision points. We interviewed a number of teachers who were at various stages in the move from traditional to portfolio assessment. Each teacher offered insights and practical solutions to how the portfolio process has worked for them. For instance, one teacher shared her letters to parents that explained the changes they would experience, as accountability would come in the form of portfolios instead of report cards only. There are also numerous examples of forms and formats for collecting portfolio data, with examples of completed forms and the disposition of information.

The book also provides strategies for designing portfolios, collecting data, making decisions about curriculum and instruction, and reporting progress. In Chapter 1, we share the history of portfolio assessment and provide workable definitions for the process and function of portfolios. Inherent in the definitions are our perceptions of learning from a constructivist perspective. This involves the environment, teacher attitudes, and the process of teacher decision making.

In Chapter 2, we cover the process of decision making based on the principles of sound portfolio assessment in more depth. Each decision point carries with it choices to be made; these are described with examples offered from actual classroom experiences.

Chapter 3 takes the decision-making framework and operationalizes the process. It guides the reader through the actual design as suggested by classroom needs. The scheduling of evidence collection and plan for managing it are discussed in an easy-to-apply manner. The chapter closes with a discussion of how to transform assessment information into decisions on behalf of students.

In Chapter 4, we focus on differentiated instruction—modifying, enhancing, and adjusting curriculum and instructional processes based on portfolio information. This is an important step, as it makes the portfolio assessment process an integral part of the curriculum and instruction process.

In the last chapter, we explore the essential concerns in implementing portfolio assessment. Each concern is addressed from a micro- and macrolevel, with examples of real solutions provided whenever possible.

The primary features that may appeal to the reader/teacher are: (1) the clear theoretical base, (2) the simple decision-making framework, (3) authentic examples of the shift to portfolio assessment as experienced by real teachers, (4) the specific application of the process as part of the Early Assessment for Exceptional Potential grant, (5) clear discussion of how teachers use portfolio data for planning and modifying curriculum, and (6) honest exploration of the barriers and concerns in implementing portfolio assessment at the classroom and schoolwide levels.

Any work of this nature would not be possible without the long-term commitment and cooperation of our field-based colleagues. Our teachers—Jenny Cos, Mary Anne Davis, and Kathy Montague—who let us peek into their classrooms and allowed us the opportunity to "think aloud" with them about the process of portfolios were invaluable assistants. Teachers from Twinsburg, Akron, and Ravenna Schools, who were part of the earliest efforts for the Early Assessment project, were among the most thoughtful, hardworking, and caring individuals with whom we have worked. They gave long hours to the design, implementation, and evaluation of the model and led us to new understandings of how alternative assessments shape teaching. To them, we extend our deepest appreciation and gratitude.

Chapter 1

On the Road
to Authentic Assessment

THINKING ABOUT IT

Mrs. Bain's Journal

8-20-96

It's been a great summer—I can't believe how fast it went! The time spent "refueling" myself as Mom, wife, daughter, and friend helped me put a bit more balance in my life. Tomorrow I'm back to work—with a new building principal and a new curriculum specialist and who knows what else! Getting to know a new group of sixth-graders is always exciting (and challenging—I wonder what the latest is this year?). What will this new administration bring? Changes in curriculum? Changes in evaluation? Changes in my classroom? Oh, well, I will soon see. Better get some sleep—I'll need it.

As each school year begins, like Mrs. Bain, all educators are faced with some unknowns: new children and families, new personnel, and sometimes new ideas. Recently, there have been exciting innovations in the area of student assessment. The concept of portfolio assessment, in particular, has been changing the way schools and teachers evaluate and report progress.

The story of designing and implementing a portfolio assessment system cannot be told without the stories of teachers and children who collaborate to understand learning and progress. Teachers have long spoken of the frustration of trying to accurately assess and report on students' progress. Further, they have decried measurement systems that put them in a position of doing *to* students instead of doing *with* students. One teacher spoke of it this way:

> *I know that I have to give tests and fill out report cards. But every time I start the process, I feel so frustrated. How can a score or grade tell you how much Jason has really learned in our classroom? He began as a shy, introverted second-grader who seldom completed his work. Now, Jason displays a keen sense of humor in his writing, engages much more often in group activities, and is "coming around." How can you grade that? There is so much more to Jason than a score or letter grade.*

Teachers, parents, and students have known for a long time how desperately the descriptions of student learning and progress need to be broadened. What teachers do in the classroom should ultimately benefit children, not punish them; there must be a better way.

The growing frustration with the current system of measuring student achievement has been further fueled by the public communications of student progress. For example, many school districts are required by the state to publish standardized tests scores. Out of context, a single measure of student performance, and perhaps not a valid one, these scores describe for the community the quality of its schools. Any teacher who has worked in a school district with low scores knows the frustration and humiliation of such publicity. The teachers also know how hard they and their students have been working, what growth and progress they have made, and the difficulties that ensue when publicizing such efforts. We often hear, "If only you knew how far they *have* come!"

The purpose of this book is not to belabor the current measurement system nor to defend poor test scores. Rather, its purpose is to describe a process of assessment that has the potential to benefit children, empower teachers, and better inform parents and community members.

HISTORY OF PORTFOLIO ASSESSMENT

In the dialogue about various forms of assessment, there is one constant. All parties agree on the need for documenting children's progress. How one defines the concept of *progress* and how one engages in the documentation are two of the points of difference. In our efforts to promote the portfolio assessment process, it is interesting to examine the trends leading to this form of assessment.

It was not until the middle of the nineteenth century that the growth and development of human beings began to be seen from a scientific perspective. As scientific inquiry into developmental processes grew, so grew the need to quantify this development. Interest in measuring all sorts of phenomena (intelligence, achievement, aptitude, personality, etc.) grew out of scientific inquiry (McAfee & Leong, 1994). The development of measures to assess psychological phenomena as well as careful observational strategies to chronicle child development emerged through the decades. Such forms of assessment added to one's understanding of individual differences. Both the testing movement and the child study movement emerged as a result of the sociopolitical times. As these factors have changed, so have the reasons for assessment.

Accountability is the present watchword tied to the process of assessment. More specifically, the educational system is held accountable by administrators, parents, legislators, and society as a whole. Perhaps issues of accountability can be described as what has driven educational reform for decades. If measurements suggest that the educational system has not accomplished its aim of preparing today's children to be tomorrow's leaders, then the citizenry searches for reforms that will correct this dilemma.

Accountability occurs at many levels, ranging from the classroom-home level to the national-legislative level. The more local level of accountability is that of classroom teachers communicating with families about their children's progress. Report cards have traditionally been the format used, with teachers assigning grades using criterion-referenced tests, standardized tests, and assorted other pieces of information. Historically, the information was unidirectional; the parents' only role was to acknowledge receipt of the report card/test scores. At the school district level, student achievement has traditionally been compiled to assess the success of the schools in educating students. Funding has been tied to such success. At the national-legislative level, far-reaching survey data have been gathered and analyzed to assess the status of education. Over the century, the roots of educational reform movements can be traced to such global forms of assessment.

The last two decades have seen a growing critique of standardized testing as the form of accountability of choice. In particular, the misuse of testing for placement or exclusion from programs for children under the age of 8 (i.e., early childhood) has been noted (Bredekamp & Rosegrant, 1992). The questions of reliability and validity of tests for young children— children from diverse ethnic and racial backgrounds as well as students with disabilities—are at the center of these critiques. In essence, the processes of assessment have been scrutinized for appropriateness and purpose. *Accountability*, consequently, has taken on a broader meaning. Teachers are accountable to themselves, their students, the families of their students, the schools, and society. As a result, teachers need assessment practices that can inform all of these constituents. Educators have been directed to choose and apply assessment practices that inform their instruction, provide individual as well as aggregated information about students, include student input, and can be communicated to multiple audiences (National Association of State Boards of Education, 1988).

Many different names have been applied to the range of innovative assessment practices that have emerged recently. There is still recognition of the value and place for more formal assessment strategies (e.g., standardized tests, criterion-referenced tests, diagnostic assessment), however. Indeed, the appropriate application of varying forms of assessment are recognized. *Authentic, assessment,* or *performance assessment,* has been the term used to describe a series of assessment practices that evaluate the child in the process of performing real tasks with relevance to his or her education (McAfee & Leong, 1994). Such performance-based, realistic, contextualized assessment may then be applied to decision making about instruction. The compilation of the information that emerges from authentic assessment over time can provide a developmental record of children's performance and progress. *Portfolio assessment,* a practical strategy for organizing such data, has emerged as a very important innovation in the scheme of assessment reform.

Portfolio assessment describes both a process and a place. The place is that of the physical collection of materials or data (e.g., writing samples, artwork), often a folder or a box. The process, on the other hand, involves multiple sources and multiple methods, over multiple points of time. The process provides rich information that goes far beyond the static numbers of standardized tests.

> ## AT A GLANCE...
> ### Authentic Assessment—Portfolio Assessment
>
> ◆ The child performs real tasks that are related to the educational process.
>
> ◆ Information is used to make decisions about curriculum and instruction.
>
> ◆ Information is collected over time, from multiple sources, and using multiple methods.
>
> ◆ It is both a process and a place.

Assessment

As previously noted in the historical overview of assessment practices, teachers have relied on quantitative forms of measurement to document how much children know about a specified area. Traditionally, quantitative measures have documented how teachers, schools, districts, and the nation have done in educating children. Though quantitative measures have given a sense of the "big picture," their value has depended on the ability to assess reliably and validly. Lacking in this tradition has been the qualitative nature of what is and what is not known. For example, a teacher might be able to note that a child scored 70 percent in mathematics, but unless that teacher has the time to take a closer look, he or she would not necessarily be able to determine where the child needs help, what concepts need to be mastered, and what instructional strategies should be used to enhance development. Consequently, teachers may be able to say that students have not met the goals, but they are at a loss as to why. On a more child-classroom level, teachers do not really know why this child failed or if the child could succeed in a different format, using different materials. Authentic assessment augments the quantitative tradition by adding a qualitative component to the assessment process. The qualitative component can help teachers answer the question: Why?

Authentic assessment contributes subjective, personal, and professional elements to the objective measures. When one includes the multiple perspectives, then there are avenues for confirming and disconfirming the more idiosyncratic views of particular children. This helps teachers know why a student can do some things well and cannot do others at all. Likewise, by including self-evaluation in the process, there are multiple points of view that add depth and richness to the assessment process as well as encourage responsibility for one's actions.

Qualitative measures do not rely on the same statistical methods that evaluate the rigor (e.g., reliability and validity) of the process. However, reliability is built in because of the multiple sources of input. Validity and generalizability are based on more locally defined standards, rubrics, and past performance. The results of qualitative assessments such as those found in portfolios are a rich, contoured image of what, when, how, and where a child has demonstrated learning. It also results in formative data for planning where, what, when, and how future activity should take place. Finally, qualitative processes place particular importance on understanding and respecting the views of others. In the case of portfolio assessment, this means the roles of teacher, student, and parent/community member become somewhat different in the portfolio process from the traditional roles assigned to them in a standardized assessment process.

In his book *Assessing Student Performance* (1993), Grant Wiggins describes assessment as a "comprehensive, multifaceted analysis of performance; it must be judgment based and personal" (p. 13). According to Wiggins, the process of assessment is a joint one in which the student and teacher are allies in the improvement of student performance. The National Association for the Education of Young Children (NAEYC) has taken a similar perspective, noting, "Assessment of individual children's development and learning is essential for planning and implementing developmentally-appropriate programs, but should be used with caution to prevent discrimination against the individual and to ensure accuracy" (Bredekamp, 1987, p. 13). The NAEYC position statement goes on to say that any assessment should be used only to benefit the child.

The characteristics of a sound assessment system have been described by many organizations and researchers (e.g., Genishi, 1992; Paulson & Paulson, 1990; Perrone, 1991; Bredekamp, 1987; Wiggins, 1993). These elements can be used as a rubric against which teachers can evaluate their own assessment systems.

AT A GLANCE...
Critical Elements of Assessment

◆ Assessment should be authentic and valid.

◆ Assessment should encompass the whole child.

◆ Assessment should involve repeated observations of various patterns of behavior.

◆ Assessment should be continuous over time.

◆ Assessment should use a variety of methods for gathering evidence of student performance.

◆ Assessment should provide a means for systematic feedback to be used in the improvement of instruction and student performance.

◆ Assessment should provide an opportunity for joint conversations and explanations between students and teachers, teachers and parents, and students and parents.

Looking at the critical elements of an assessment system does not translate it into answering the practical question: What do I do in my classroom if I want to design and implement this type of framework for assessing student performance? Before answering this question, one must consider how students learn and how teachers can create environments to maximize learning.

Assumptions about Learning

The professional and personal knowledge of teaching is rooted in theory, research, and personal understandings of teachers. The understanding of theory and research is embedded in teachers' applications and interpretations of their teaching practices. When teachers practice their teaching, their beliefs, values, and attitudes about children's ways of learning become a necessary focal point when considering actual teaching strategies and procedures. Because of the need to integrate theory and research with personal experiences of teachers, an understanding of major orientation is necessary to consolidate one's own beliefs about how children learn, in what ways teachers should teach, and the role of assessment in the process. This book embraces one particular perspective of how children learn and how teachers teach: constructivism. Constructivism is rooted in the work of John Dewey, Jean Piaget, Lev Vygotsky, and Lawrence Kohlberg.

The constructivist approach proposes that children learn by interacting in their environment as active agents who build, or construct, personal understandings of their experiences. Learning in school settings is viewed as the interaction between teacher, students, and the actual learning resources and experiences intentionally, and unintentionally, planned within the school environment. Within the parameters of constructivism, learning for understanding occurs through a student's desire for active meaning making. Through active involvement, the child continually engages in learning experiences and synthesizes new experiences with what was previously learned. The construction of emergent understandings and relationships is crystallized when compared with previously held ideas and beliefs. This requires the teacher to understand, prior to planning and presentation of appropriate learning experiences, what the child knows and what the child has experienced.

From a constructivist perspective, the teacher is constantly considering the student's point of view (e.g., actual understanding, his or her construction of meaning) when thinking about curriculum development, instructional strategies, and assessment procedures. The teacher focuses on what the child can actually demonstrate and explores the student's current and emerging abilities from the student's understanding rather than the teacher's understanding. In other words, the teacher becomes concerned about what the child actually knows and understands as opposed to the child trying to understand the correct or conventional adult understanding. For example, when a teacher approaches learning to read from a constructivist orientation, he or she must first observe and learn what a child knows before considering what materials and instructional strategies are necessary. The constructivist-oriented teacher assumes the child knows many things about reading; the teacher's response is to value that by asking the child to demonstrate his or her knowledge through varied classroom activities. Through functional, meaning-making activities, the teacher builds on what the child previously knows by *scaffolding* new experiences that will promote emerging and new learnings. The teacher's responsibility is much like a partner, who considers what the child knows and offers sound opportunities to expand his or her understandings (Bredekamp & Rosegrant, 1992).

Robert Allen—Kindergarten

Robert is a constructivist teacher. Before he plans appropriate instructional opportunities, he believes that it is important for him to find out what a child knows. Therefore, Robert has given all of his kindergartners an informal inventory of words and sounds. He has determined that some children know that certain letters make certain sounds. Joshua, for example, recognized *MOM* by both sounds and letters. Robert asked Joshua to look around the room to see if there are any other *M* words in the classroom. Joshua pointed out Melissa and Makita's names on their lunchboxes, the word *music* at the music center, and the word *mailbox* at the writing center.

A constructivist orientation for authentic assessment is important because it allows the teacher to meaningfully plan, implement, and assess students' learning. It allows the teacher to predict possible reactions to the classroom environment, to detect barriers to learning, and to identify which elements contribute to student learning. Through careful observation and interaction with students, the teacher is able to focus on the actual understandings that the child has constructed and learned. Furthermore, the teacher can provide authentic learning experiences that are personalized for the student. As opposed to "covering" the curriculum and modeling "frontal teaching" (e.g., teaching as telling), the teacher provides ample opportunity for exploring, examining, and discussing in a wide variety of venues (e.g., small group, large group, individualized). Finally, a constructivist perspective focuses the teacher on assessment strategies that provide an accurate view of what a child

---

AT A GLANCE...
Assumptions about Constructivist Learning

◆ Students learn by interacting with their environment.

◆ Students have a basic need to make meaning out of their experiences.

◆ Students need to be actively involved with resources and ideas.

◆ New ideas emerge when students compare their experiences with old ideas and experiences.

◆ The teacher must be aware of what a student already knows and understands and build the new learning from present knowledge.

◆ Students engage in exploring, examining, discussing, and learning new ideas and concepts in large, small, and individual groups.

---

knows and how he or she knows it through the use of observation, anecdotal records, student products, and conferencing with students and parents.

Environment

A classroom that is truly constructivist, truly sensitive to students, will look quite different from the traditional classroom. In a constructivist classroom, the curriculum and the environment are inextricably intertwined. The curriculum *is* the environment. The engagement of the student in real, relevant, hands-on activity means the student is constantly interacting with the environment.

The environmental components are more than the furniture, the layout of the room, the spatial arrangement, the time schedule, and the interpersonal interactions with adults and peers (Bersani & Barbour, 1991). Choices of content and curriculum to be covered are also environmental components. Nothing is left to chance and everything is there for a purpose. For instance, if students are expected to work in cooperative learning groups, then the spatial arrangement must allow for flexibility and reconfiguration of space. If, as one teacher noted, children learn to talk by speaking, not keeping silent, then verbal interaction becomes a major element in the environment. As one looks at each of the environmental components in relation to the climate necessary for authentic assessment, it becomes clearer how the constructivist approach supports the process.

The materials and equipment that one would find in a constructivist environment (i.e., one in which authentic assessment informs curriculum and instruction) would be those that stimulate the learner to engage in manipulation, construction, deconstruction, and experimentation. Two-dimensional materials will not suffice, nor will single models or materials. Such materials do not allow for individual meaning making, schema building, or knowledge generation. Consequently, materials and equipment that can be manipulated, consumed, taken apart, and constructed are those that would facilitate constructive learning and alternative assessment. For instance, we have seen "fix-it" centers in preschool and elementary-level classrooms where children can take apart old appliances (with the electrical cords removed, of course) to see what makes them tick.

The spatial arrangement, as already noted, should be flexible, facilitate interactions with others, and allow for display of work-in-progress. Many meaningful learning experiences cannot be completed in one session or even one day. Likewise, there is great value in revisiting earlier thinking about a concept in order to revise ideas. This also suggests the need for display and documentation that can be easily accessed. Finally, portfolio products take up space that must be readily available to students and adults for the ongoing process to be practical.

The time component is also critical in a constructivist classroom and is often the one most controlled by external guidelines. There are some immutable aspects, such as lunch schedules and special classes; however, there are scheduling traditions that defy an integrated approach to learning. Consequently, schedules should not be defined by content areas when possible. Instead, a schedule that is open and built around the immutable parts (e.g., literacy development) allows for in-depth explorations, integration of content, and ongoing projects. All are elements of a constructivist classroom.

The interpersonal interactions in such an environment can occur only when all of these other pieces are in place. The other critical element in this scenario is the attitude of the teacher that interpersonal interactions are important to the learning process—that conferencing time is as valuable as instructional time. Certainly, an authentic assessment process such as portfolio assessment cannot happen when multiple levels of interactions are not encouraged. Opportunities for small group, whole group, individual learning as well as student/teacher conferencing or peer editing all provide the multiple interactions needed for student growth and development. Time for these interactions, space for these interactions, and valuing of these interactions are critical elements in this environment.

In order to establish a portfolio assessment system, the environment of the classroom has to be designed to facilitate active student learning. Such environmental considerations are evident in Mrs. Adams's description of her constructivist-based classroom. After three years of conducting portfolio assessment, Mrs. Adams spoke about it this way:

When I first started portfolio assessment, I found it difficult to collect a variety of pieces of evidence. I just wasn't getting anything, except worksheets, from the kids. I began to realize that if the children weren't actively engaged in creating their own knowledge, in making choices and decisions, in selecting opportunities to display what they know…that the only evidence I would collect would be what I always got, really what I gave out. I had to learn to step out of the teacher as director of instruction and into the teacher as facilitator of learning.

The classroom environment is crucial to the design and implementation of a portfolio assessment system. Wiggins (1993) echoes this concern when he comments that teachers need to create assessment systems that are "respectful" of the students they serve. He notes that when a person is respectful of others, he or she is open with them about his or her methods and purposes (i.e., no hidden agenda or surprise tests). The respectful person allows others to explain or clarify their answers if he or she does not understand. Further, the respectful person gives feedback to others and provides ample opportunities for them to refine and master skills (Wiggins, 1993).

Mrs. Trivelli's classroom can present another view of an environment that engages children in active learning. When entering the room, a number of small and large group areas are seen, as well as learning centers with hands-on activities and individual niches for students' three-dimensional projects. On the side of the room is a large cabinet with a file drawer labeled "Student Portfolios." As part of an active learning environment, students are encouraged to talk, explain their thinking, and engage others in conversation. "After all," Mrs. Trivelli said, "Children develop language by speaking, not by being silent." Mrs. Trivelli's curriculum, and subsequently her instructional techniques, give children authentic choices and decisions to make about their learning. Further, she has some activities designed for the whole class and some for smaller segments of the class. Her classroom practices reflect the knowledge that she has gained about student strengths and progress through portfolio assessment and her belief in constructivist principles of learning.

If this is the kind of environment that engages students in the construction of knowledge, then what is the role of the teacher? Following are some comments from teachers who use this approach:

My whole teaching process has changed during the past five years. We successfully use specific learning experiences to meet needs and learning styles of individual students. I am more conscientious about evaluating student performance on personal/individual growth rather than compared to the "norm." I am more conscientious about evaluating student performance in a variety of ongoing ways—not a weekly paper and pencil test. (Pugliese, 7/8th grade, 1995)

I am more aware of how I ask questions and the answers I am eliciting from students. We are not always looking for one right answer or any answer at all. We are less book conscious. (Gallagher, 5th grade, 1995)

These examples illustrate how teachers move out of the direct instructional role and into more of a facilitation role in a constructivist environment. Does this mean that students get to learn anything they want? No, but it does mean that students are offered a variety of ways to "show what they know" and that teachers use a variety of ways to document and assess student progress.

Finally, it appears that an integrated or thematic approach to curriculum supports both constructivism and the use of portfolio assessment. Much has been written regarding integrated curriculum approaches (e.g., Bredekamp & Rosegrant, 1992; Jacobs, 1989; Spodek & Saracho, 1994; VanTassel-Baska, 1994). Several notions support the need for an integrated approach to the curriculum for students. Jacobs (1989) states these issues most clearly:

1. *Growth of Knowledge:* Teachers cannot keep up with the tremendous rate of information and knowledge that is being discovered. Further, students cannot make sense of such amounts of information in isolation. Teachers need to help students see how things, ideas, facts fit together in our world.

2. *Fragmentation of Schedules:* Many schools move students through their day in 42-minute intervals. As one teacher put it, "I have about 20 minutes of real teaching after the kids get settled and before they mentally, if not physically, leave." This means that students receive less instruction, more fragmentation, and lack of depth of understanding in their classwork. Teachers who work in interdisciplinary teams focus their efforts on establishing the linkages, providing depth, and decreasing fragmentation through integrated planning.

3. *Relevance of Curriculum:* An age-old question from students is: What does this have to do with real life?

Too little teaching and selection of content is relevant to the day-to-day lives of students. Further, teachers, in general, are failing to make the bridge between what students are learning and what they need to know to live. Integrated curriculum provides students with a continuum of learning activities that reflect authentic experiences. For example, instead of writing a traditional thank-you note, as listed in the English textbook, teachers tie the writing process to an authentic experience (e.g., writing a note of appreciation to the guest speaker on Native American artifacts).

AT A GLANCE...
A Portfolio Assessment Environment

◆ The teacher is a facilitator of the environment—planning, organizing, assessing, and modifying as the need arises.

◆ The students are actively engaged in learning—moving around, discussing ideas with each other, exploring, asking questions, and suggesting new ideas.

◆ The curriculum is integrated rather than organized around separate content areas: Themes and interdisciplinary topics are the organizing elements, and ideas are connected.

An examination of the environment that facilitates portfolio assessment reveals three major components: teachers as facilitators, students engaged in active learning, and an integrated curriculum. When these elements are in place, assessment is a natural outgrowth of classroom work.

Teacher Attitudes

Another key element to the use of portfolios relates to teacher perception and attitude. O'Brien (1993) draws on the work of others in this area who suggest that teachers develop educational environments that are aligned with their own personal perspectives. O'Brien (1993) writes:

> *Because teachers interpret curriculum prescriptions and other programmatic emphases in different ways due to their implicit beliefs, theory does not automatically transfer to practice. Deep-seated cultural beliefs influence how teachers perceive classroom situations and interpret the educational setting. Included in teacher beliefs is a set of values about what teachers and children ought to do in school settings and what children ought to learn. (p. 5)*

In other words, what a teacher believes about children influences both what the teacher offers to them and what the teacher accepts from them. In our work with classroom teachers, we have found that teachers involved in portfolio assessment change their perceptions of the children with whom they work (Viechnicki, Barbour, Shaklee, Rohrer, & Ambrose, 1993). For example, when working with children from poverty settings, if a teacher believes that children of poverty cannot be gifted, then no matter what assessment system is used, traditional or alternative, the teacher will still not "see" the child as gifted.

Once a teacher has examined what he or she believes about children and has identified his or her own biases or barriers, then that teacher is ready to become a systematic and objective observer of a child's talents and abilities. As one teacher noted, "I think I see more different facets in children and realize that they can be learning disabled and still be gifted" and "I try to be more observant of the children and listen to even the small things. They could be important clues." The teacher clears the lenses through which he or she views children.

In order to examine the limitations teachers place on students and expectations for student performance, a systematic and thorough plan of staff development should be part of a systemwide implementation of portfolio assessment. This is not to suggest, however, that a single teacher cannot implement portfolios in his or her individual classroom. Whether one is looking at a systemwide implementation or an individual implementation, a teacher should first examine what he or she believes about children, who they are, and what they should be doing.

Finally, teachers who use portfolio assessment in the classroom should also be aware and sensitive of the cultures within which their students live. The selection of activities or experiences should be designed to give children the opportunity to share their cultural heritages in positive and meaningful ways. For example, portfolio assessment models that rely heavily on written examples may not capture the rich heritage of a child who follows an oral tradition of sharing. Sensitive and aware teachers provide a wide variety of ways in which to capture a child's learning.

AT A GLANCE...
Teachers' Perceptions and Attitudes about Students and Assessment

◆ Teachers examine their own beliefs and attitudes; they "clear the lenses."

◆ Teachers see children as individuals, each with a unique set of potentials and abilities.

◆ Teachers discard the traditional "deficit" models; they focus on what students can do rather than on what they cannot do.

◆ Teachers are aware of the many ways students and families communicate information, and they provide an opportunity to use those ways in the classroom.

◆ Teachers believe that students can and will accept responsibility for learning; they work to encourage students to accept responsibilities congruent with their age and stage of development.

Usability of Information

Another major factor in the issue of portfolio assessment relates to the usability of the evidence collected about each student. A teacher who constructs a portfolio assessment approach for his or her classroom must be cautious about exchanging that information in a meaningful way with other classrooms or teachers. Although it can be an excellent tool for assessing student progress within a class, if there is no standardization or joint staff development, the information is less meaningful in the broader context of school.

For example, if you construct a portfolio based on student writing skills and, as an individual teacher, you decide which skills to focus on, what products will be collected to represent "best evidence" of those skills, and how often you will ask for contributions from students, that does not necessarily mean that your colleague across the hall teaching the same grade level would agree with anything you have done. He may decide that the level of skills is too high or too low. He might not agree that the products collected were the "best evidence" of a student's skills, and/or he might not think that students can really select their own "best evidence." Without such joint agreements and understandings that can be established through systematic staff development, portfolios are relevant and usable only in our individual classrooms (Shaklee & Viechnicki, 1994).

The Difference between Portfolio Assessment and Portfolio Collection

One of the critical issues in portfolio assessment is to be able to distinguish between a collection of work that is placed in a folder and called a portfolio and an assessment model designed to monitor and enhance student performance in the classroom. Several key elements should be embedded in the design of the portfolio itself if it is to be used for assessment of student abilities and/or progress (see Figure 1–1).

The first element that should be identifiable is clear, specific, research-based criteria for student assessment. These criteria can be based on national standards (e.g., National Council of Teachers of Mathematics [NCTM]) that describe the acquisition of specific content understandings or developmental frameworks that describe the expectations for student development with regard to specific domains (National Association for the Education of Young Children [NAEYC]). Furthermore, the national standards might be incorporated into the state standards

Portfolios

Collection --- *Assessment*

Why am I collecting evidence?	How am I using the evidence?
• For representative skills	• To offer the next level
• For areas of development	• To promote development
• For demonstrated ability	• To document ability
• For conferencing	• To modify instruction
• For reporting	• To adapt curriculum

FIGURE 1–1 *Decision Making Based on Evidence*

document and enfolded into the district course of study. The linkage between and among standards is important to the overall design of a portfolio assessment system. As a classroom teacher, you might use the course of study for social studies to design a portfolio assessment model. In the broader scheme of thinking, your portfolio assessment model could be linked to the state standard and into the national recommendations if the intent is to use this alternative system for all students in your district.

As one reviews the local course of study or other frameworks for thinking about portfolio assessment, the criteria listed should be translated into specific observable behaviors that the teacher, student, and parent can understand. For example, in education for gifted children, occasionally a checklist of behaviors will include: "Child engages in flights of fantasy." What does that look like in your classroom? Can you really tell the difference between a child looking out of a window at a bird and a child looking out of the same window engaged in a flight of fantasy? The same is true of other criteria. When examining the research-based descriptions of how a child gains the skills of literacy, for instance, or any other area, you should be able to discuss with your team what that looks like in your classroom. What observations can you make? What products can you collect or what activities can you design that would encourage students to demonstrate their knowledge and acquisition of the criteria?

A second element that should be embedded in a portfolio assessment design is the notion of using multiple sources of information to make an assessment of a child's skills and/or abilities. Three areas should be considered:

(1) persons who can contribute information, (2) different methods that can be used to collect information, and (3) different sources of information. Looking at specific examples in each of these areas should be helpful. People who know the child well are potential contributors to the assessment process. Typically, a classroom teacher and the student are the sole contributors to the portfolio. However, there are others who also know the student very well; parents and/or guardians, community members, other building teachers or administrators, classmates, or resource specialists have the potential to contribute meaningful and relevant information to the assessment process. It is not unusual to begin with just two people contributing to a portfolio, but future plans should include incorporating other people into the assessment process.

Continuing the design of sound portfolio assessment models, you should also consider the different methods by which information (i.e., evidence) can be contributed to the portfolio. These methods could include both print and nonprint evidence (e.g., audio/videotape), observations/anecdotal records, self-reports, and peer evaluations, to name a few. Further, as a portfolio is reviewed, the materials should also include a variety of sources of data. In this case, consider a variety of places (e.g., in class, at recess, in special classes) and times of day/year in which the information is collected. This permits you to view each child throughout the day as well as throughout the year, in different settings, to determine under what circumstances a child manifests certain skills or abilities. For example, if you were assessing leadership skills, you might observe not only within your cooperative learning activities but also during social activities (e.g., on the playground). If you consistently record evidence of leadership ability on the playground but not in the classroom, then you might want to consider engaging this student more specifically in leadership activities in an academic setting.

AT A GLANCE...
Portfolios as Assessment Tools

◆ The plan for portfolio assessment should have clearly stated and observable criteria for making judgments.

◆ A portfolio contains information from those who know the student well, such as parents/guardians, family members, teachers, resource specialists, and so on.

◆ A portfolio has many different types of information—for example, writing samples, tests, drawings, audio/videotapes.

◆ A portfolio is added to on a regular basis over the school year.

◆ Portfolios can look very different from one program to another, depending on the purpose and intent.

◆ Portfolios are open and available to teachers, parents/family members, and students.

Of all the key elements that make a portfolio an assessment plan rather than simply a collection of student work is the process that is employed to modify classroom practices and curriculum based on evidence found within a portfolio. The evidence within the portfolio becomes a planning tool for teachers and students to make decisions to enhance and develop a student's skills and abilities. The evaluation of the information collected and the decisions made on behalf of the student are specifically identified and clearly documented. At the conclusion of the experience, a review of the decisions is made with a focus on continuation, change, or affirmation that these particular strategies or curricular experiences made a contribution to the child's development (see Figure 1–2).

The following chapters will highlight specific decision-making points and provide examples of ways in which a wide variety of teachers are considering the portfolio assessment process. Although there is no "right" way to conduct portfolio assessment, taking the time to plan, examining specific strategies, and using timelines from other teachers may help you in creating a viable portfolio assessment model for your classroom.

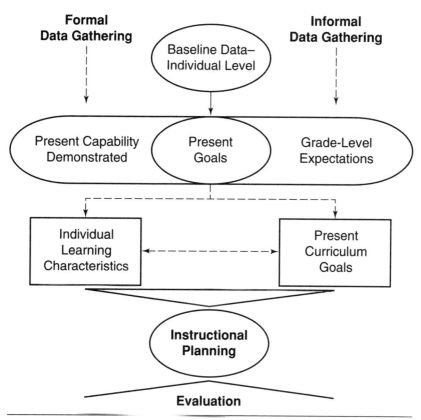

FIGURE 1–2 *Decision-Making Framework*

Chapter 2

Portfolio Assessment as a Decision-Making Process

THINKING ABOUT IT
Mrs. Bain's Journal

8-30-96

The word is out—we need to move toward authentic assessment methods. Our curriculum specialist is pushing it and the ad hoc curriculum committee has already put together a checklist from our graded course of study so that we can keep track of what we have that is authentic evidence that demonstrates the child's performance on that objective. How am I ever going to be able to keep track of what every child is doing in all of the pupil performance objectives? I already take home a box of work every night. My kids think I care more about the students than I do about them. My husband says I don't get paid enough to

*work an 80-hour week. Maybe I can get some ideas
from some of the other primary teachers.*

9-3-96

*Okay, so when I sit down at grading time, what is it
that I think about when I determine grades in each
subject for each kid? I have some test and quiz scores.
I also try to recall how they have done in individual
reading and writing activities, but I don't have those
pieces of evidence in front of me. Geez, its hard to
remember what Sam has done—he's always so quiet
and compliant. So maybe there is something to be
said about having hard evidence to look at when I'm
making my decisions. I sure do need them when I
refer a kid to special ed. In the in-service session,
Sally asked me how I knew whether I was planning
instruction that was meeting every child's needs. The
truth is, I don't know. I think about where most of
them are functioning and I go for it—but then sometimes Susan is bored to tears and other times Jeanie
is ready to cry because she can't follow what's going
on. I do the best I can to hit everyone's level. How can
I possibly figure out what each child needs and plan
for it? Nothing in my training helped me learn how
to do this. I mean, can anybody really do this? How
am I ever going to pull all of this together—there's
only one of me.*

9-8-96

Well, I guess some of my grade-level colleagues are getting "into" this authentic assessment stuff. They were talking about it at our grade-level meeting today. Someone went to a presentation about portfolio assessment—a process for doing authentic assessment. He had some interesting ideas about how to put the materials together—empty boxes, file cabinet space. I guess that could hold quite a bit of stuff and you stack it up pretty compactly—but what do I put in it and how do I choose things that will make sense later on? Carol says she's been choosing one piece of writing for each kid each week so that she can look for progress. But what should she look for?

As Mrs. Bain's journal shows, she is struggling with the new expectations from her building administrators to make her assessments more authentic. She is not alone. The challenge to shift to new strategies entails many decisions and changes. Consequently, the decision to use a portfolio assessment process may be a major shift in operating for many teachers. Typical comments include: "I don't have time to keep track of all the students!" "How do I assign grades/make decisions about placement?" "How do I account for meeting all of the district's grade-level objectives?" There are, of course, no easy answers to these questions except to say that the process has worked for many teachers. But the decision to use portfolio assessment is just the first in a long line of decisions necessary in this process.

There are three dimensions to all the decisions that one makes about portfolio assessment, as described in Paulson and Paulson's (1990) article: (1) *the activity dimension,* which involves decisions about the rationale, intentions, contents, standards, and judgments for the portfolio; (2) *the historical dimension,* including the necessary conditions prior to, the process over time, and the end conditions; and (3) *the stakeholders* in the assessment process, those for whom the assessment has meaning. The actual portfolio process can, and does, take on different shapes, depending on how each of the dimensions is defined.

For instance, the activity dimension may be defined as the need to identify young children with developmental delays in all domains. The rationale, intentions, contents, standards, and judgments would focus on the assessment of the child's developmental level of functioning in all domains. The contents of the portfolio might consist of developmental observations, checklists, anecdotal records, a developmental questionnaire completed by the parents, and a developmental screening measure. The portfolio contents might be gathered over a period of six months and then evaluated against developmental information in the form of norms and observations. Judgments about the need for special placement and services would be made based on the evaluation of the entire portfolio.

Other examples might look quite different based on the rationale or purpose for the portfolio. Additional examples that are evident in the literature include portfolios for assessing emergent reading and writing, mathematics, and exceptional potential, or schoolwide portfolios that assess student contributions in citizenship, academics, and service.

DECISIONS BEFORE BEGINNING

Decision 1: What Will It Look Like? What Are the Purposes?

The primary concern is the purpose that the portfolio will serve. The best way of explaining this is to focus your attention on the other professions that have traditionally used portfolios. Artists have long used portfolios to demonstrate the development, quantity, and quality of their work. Included in an artist's portfolio might be examples of her or his artwork; documentation of training, awards, or gallery showings; works in progress; and future plans for works. If the medium is three dimensional, then there may be photographs or slides of works. The artist's purpose in sharing the portfolio may determine the contents. If the artist is hoping to get a show in a gallery, then the focus may be on other shows he or she has had. In any case, the artist is dependent on the representativeness of his or her work and the standards of the gallery for the subsequent decisions. The same would be true for other professions who employ portfolio assessment, such as writers, architects, jewelers, and woodworkers.

Purpose or rationale for the portfolio is considered part of the activity dimension of the process according to Paulson and Paulson (1990). This decision is the one defining the "philosophical basis and operational guidelines for collecting materials and placing them in the portfolio" (p. 70). For the teacher, it is important to determine what the purpose of the portfolio will be. If it is to serve as the source for evaluating overall student performance, then it will be comprehensive in nature. More specifically, will the portfolio be used as data to inform instruction? To report progress? To identify special needs? For program accountability? For all of these? Should it include a student's best work, typical work, or all types of work?

Jenny Cos—Kindergarten

Jenny Cos is a kindergarten teacher in a laboratory school. She has used portfolios as the core of her assessment process. Jenny's classroom can be described as truly child sensitive and as a model of emergent curriculum with the curriculum flowing from the ideas, interests, and assessed needs of her children. Since this in an inclusionary program, the range of abilities among her children is quite broad. Jenny views the portfolio much like one would view a photo album. It contains examples of the children's best efforts, in both the children's opinion and Jenny's opinion. She chose to use a portfolio assessment strategy because it "is an individualized procedure...no two looked the same...problem solving and creative work would be in there."

Mary Anne Davis—Second Grade

The promise of meaningful assessment has always been an integral component of Mary Anne's thinking when considering evaluating and reporting children's learning, development, and growth. Currently a second-grade teacher, Mary Anne is "experimenting" with using portfolios in her classroom. She notes that her interest in changing some of her assessment procedures dates back to two years ago when she began "collecting information on children…notes from home, children's work samples, important papers…everything" and discovered that the information she collected gave her a better sense of the children's progress and development than the traditional checklists and quarterly report cards she had been using for the past 18 years.

There is no correct answer about which work to choose, except that it should reflect the established selection criteria. Both Jenny and Mary Anne decided to use portfolios to assess the children in their respective classrooms. For each of them, this method of authentic assessment met a need to provide a rich, meaningful assessment of the students in their charge.

Each teacher, however, came to the decision to use portfolios from a different place in their careers. Jenny is a relatively new teacher who brings no previously imposed public school structure to her teaching. She sees portfolio assessment as the only way she can record the progress of her kindergartners in a complete and meaningful manner. Reflecting her philosophy, she chooses the children's best efforts. Mary Anne, on the other hand, has spent a number of years (23 to be exact) trying to fully document her second-graders' progress only to feel as if it fell short of her need to tell the full story. For both Jenny and Mary Anne, the rationale for their choice has to do with a need for telling the whole story (see Figures 2–1 and 2–2).

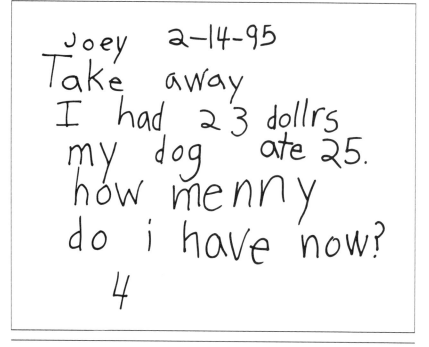

FIGURE 2–1 *Joey's Math Portfolio Entry: Second Grade*

Moltabacation is something that if you said 11 times 4. Now this is what I would do to figur this problem out. Now only on the 11's when I said 3 you Just 30 + 3 mor =33. And that gives you the answer. On 1 You add 1 × 1 = 2 ~~was can~~ On the 2's add 2 × 2 = 4 on 3 add 3 × 3 = 9 on 4's 4 × 4 = 8 on 5's 5 × 5 = 25 All you have to do is 12 × 12 you

(continued)

FIGURE 2–2 *Shannon's Math Portfolio Entry: Second Grade*

Just have 12 feet and add 12 + 12 = 24 Because 12 + 12 = 24 that is a esey way to do it. But 12 × 4 = you add 12's 4 time to 12's is 24 and then ~~add~~ Add 12 again 24 again but ~~the~~ then add 24 + 24 = 48. Because 2 and 2 is 4 and 4 + 4 is eight.

FIGURE 2-2 *(Continued)*

Decision 2: Who Should Be Involved? Who Are the Stakeholders?

This decision addresses the dimension of stakeholders. Although teachers are excellent sources of input, they are not the only source of input available. This area has been neglected in recent educational history. There are multiple sources of input available to educators—sources that are valuable informants. The sources are those who also have a stake in the student's present and future: parents/guardians, support professionals (e.g., therapists, counselors, teachers of special areas), classmates, and the student.

Teachers have many opportunities to add information to the portfolio. Special teachers (e.g., art, music, physical education) and support professionals such as counselors can provide information about students as they function in a different context than that of the regular classroom. Such input also provides information about areas other than traditionally academic ones.

Parents have usually been viewed as the recipients of data rather than a source of information. Teachers often get parent input upon enrollment in a program but rarely do they look to parents as sources of ongoing information. And yet, parents are very knowledgeable about their children. Parents often observe behaviors that are relevant to the assessment process but they have no regular process for providing such data. Further, unlike traditional forms of assessment, portfolio assessment models invest in the development of parent/teacher/student partnerships for learning. Questionnaires, parent interviews, and journals are all methods for gathering parent/guardian input.

Though a less obvious source, classmates may be able to provide input about other classmates on some areas of assessment. For instance, in assessing exceptional potential in young children, we asked classmates to name those whom they believed held expert status in specific domains: who drew the best, who asked interesting questions, who learned things quickly (Shaklee et al., 1990). Children in first grade and older were quite capable of assessing their classmates' skills. Peers as stakeholders may be appropriate for some portfolios yet not for others.

Finally, the student is a critical stakeholder in the portfolio assessment process as well as a decision maker about who the stakeholders will be. The student is the only "player" who figures in all phases of the process: subject of assessment, source of input, evaluator of data, and recipient of evaluation. The portfolio assessment literature underscores the importance of the child learning how to be an accurate self-evaluator as a result of this process. Students are expected to choose items for the portfolio on a regular basis and to be able to define why they have chosen them. They are an integral part of the evaluation of progress and performance. Although it is easier to imagine a high school student evaluating his or her essay, young children are also capable of articulating their reasons for choosing certain items.

The cast of stakeholders may vary from program to program or from teacher to teacher and from time to time. The important factor is that teachers and students define a series of multiple stakeholders in order to provide a broad panorama of the students' abilities. The overarching principle guiding this decision is to choose stakeholders based on what each has to share and what each needs to know. Implicit in the array of stakeholders is the need to maintain confidentiality.

Jenny Cos

At the beginning of the kindergarten year, Jenny keeps a keen observer's eye on the classroom, noting what individual children can and cannot do. She chooses one recording sheet that everyone has completed and makes copies to put in the portfolio so that each child has a baseline of information. She also conducts a group activity in which the children tell her what their expectations about the kindergarten experience are: "They can say either the things that they know will happen in kindergarten or the things they wish would happen... fearful or wishful. Some kids will say 'We have to sit at the desk' and another will say, 'I wish we could make a castle.' That tells me a lot about what's going on with the kids."

After a month or so, Jenny begins an individual inventory of each child. "I do it as a special thing that I do with each person in my office...to get to know them. Nothing pressured, sort of a special time. I have a special box with cards and letters and ask them to point to letters." In the process of talking and asking the children to follow specific directions, Jenny feels that she has captured her students' present levels of functioning. She uses this information to plan specific goals for individuals, focusing on the concepts and skills that she sees.

Mary Anne Davis

Mary Anne became fascinated with considering other means for assessing children's growth and thus became an avid reader of books focusing on portfolio assessment. In addition to reading, she has taken a workshop on portfolio development and use, attended the National Council of Teaching Mathematics annual conference, and collaborates regularly with a university professor in teacher education. Mary Anne begins the school year by inviting professionals from the community to share their portfolio use along with the how and why these individuals selected what to include in their professional portfolios. Mary Anne will subsequently use this activity to scaffold another activity that will occur later in the school year when children are asked to discuss with each other why they included certain pieces in their school portfolios. The students are asked to include a "worst" example of the work with examples of their "best" work in order to examine attributes that they use when determining the selection of portfolio pieces.

Jenny and Mary Anne are both new to the process of portfolio assessment and are just beginning to explore who they can rely on for information. The first thing they have done is to expand their reliance on themselves as data sources. They chose strategies for collecting information that are not typical classroom methods. Second, they have looked to the students as reliable and important informants about their own work. Already, they have moved into the realm of authentic assessment.

Decision 3: What Should Be Assessed? What Do I Need to Know?

The *what* of this decision-making process needs to be clearly tied to purpose. The infinite possibilities that abound for what might be part of the portfolio necessitate limiting that which will be included. A portfolio that documents reading and writing will look quite different from a portfolio that assesses developmental delay. The choices are endless; the choices are also critical so that meaning can be made from the contents.

The types of assessments that might be included can range from formal measures (standardized tests, norm referenced tests) to informal measures (observations, anecdotal records). Wolfgang and Wolfgang (1992) describe these choices about data gathering on a continuum from open to closed. Open methods involve no selectivity and require no inference. The most open-ended methods would be observation and teacher diaries. Closed methods involve high selectivity and high levels of inference. On the closed end of the continuum, you would find criterion-referenced tests and time sampling. The child-centered or open methods would be considered the more authentic forms of assessment, whereas the closed or teacher-centered methods would focus on specific skills. Choices about methods will relate to the purpose of the assessment.

Traditionally, schools have required teachers to use a very unbalanced plan for assessment. Choices have been between contextualized (based on classroom activity) measures such as teacher-made tests, checklists, and rating scales, and decontextualized (based on norms) measures such as standardized tests. Observations of process and observations of product have been lacking. Sampling from all of these strategies can provide a rounded perspective of the students' abilities. Additionally, the classroom context will be an integral part of the assessment process.

The answers for Jenny and Mary Anne to these questions will necessarily be different, given their different grade levels. They also have different structures for accountability. Nonetheless, they each thought carefully about what was to be assessed. They have chosen to address this question gradually. Jenny assesses a few areas at a time, relying on the children's input quite heavily. Mary Anne also begins slowly and includes all of the students in the process.

Decision 4: How Will the Assessment Be Accomplished? When Will It All Take Place?

This decision encompasses all of the pragmatic aspects of assessment. It has been established that assessment needs to be authentic, valid, ongoing, and long term, and it must encompass the whole child. Additionally, a series of other stakeholders in this process who can contribute

Jenny Cos

In the middle of the year, Jenny does what she calls a self-assessment. Using symbols to indicate how a child feels about different areas ("Things I like to read..."), she interviews each child across a range of topics. Jenny believes she not only gets the child's self-assessment of these issues but she also gets a feel for who can read the questions, write the answers, and provide detail. She uses the information "to get a sense of how they feel about things. I know then if someone likes to go to dramatic play every day but doesn't like to have to go to the other center activities.... I [may not] necessarily know why. That child may not have isolated for me that math is what [he or she doesn't] like to do. I then try to make it more interesting and engaging." Jenny also gathers information about the children's progress through the course of everyday activities. She makes an effort to record an anecdotal note on every child at least every other week. Her notes are stored in the portfolio, and at the end of the semester, she prepares an anecdotal summary for each child as a way of documenting progress. Her observations center on emerging literacy, math, problem solving, and creativity.

Mary Anne Davis

Mary Anne describes her teaching as becoming more student sensitive, where the students' points of view in what they are learning becomes much more important than simply "mastering" content and specific skills. Mary Anne describes this connection in this manner, "For example, each morning the students have a reflection period to decide what should go into their portfolio.... They are asked to consider if this piece of work shows that they know something or are using good strategies. It's better for the children; they need to know that when they complete their work that they are responsible for being self-evaluative, [to] look at their own abilities and why they engaged in certain activities." Mary Anne is also planning for the next step—the use of peer evaluation in the selection of portfolio pieces.

to portfolio development have been named. Assessment is not meant to be a one-shot tally of the students' capabilities and progress. Rather, it is meant to be an integral part of the daily classroom routine. For those new to the process, this can sound overwhelming. Classroom teachers already have more than enough to do. However, keep in mind that many teachers are already doing much of what this book advocates, although not always in a systematic and planful way.

A timeline for data gathering is essential. For some components of the portfolio, the timeline will indicate critical points in the academic year: beginning, middle, and end of year. For other components, a schedule of regular data gathering may be daily, weekly, and monthly. The timing of when products are to be selected and by whom will be another critical point. How products and other items are to be filed and housed are important factors in managing classroom space. Teachers have used pizza boxes, shoe boxes, manila folders, envelopes, file cabinets, computer disks, and cubby space to hold products over time. As in the preceding example of Jenny's classroom, a schedule for anecdotal record keeping was a daily one. The logistics of this task might include a clipboard of sheets of large mailing labels available in the classroom. As Jenny sees something noteworthy, she takes the clipboard and writes the note, dating it and adding the child's initials. Filing of the anecdotal notes occurs once a week.

The shift from one style of assessment to another (or to any innovation) requires teachers to rethink how they use the available resources, especially time and people. The inclusion of stakeholders means that there are additional people to assist. Students, in particular, are an integral part of the process. One of the goals of authentic assessment is to help students learn to be effective self-evaluators. Consequently, the assessment process does not need to be secretive anymore. Students can and should be aware of their evaluations as well as participants in them. Filing, updating, and maintaining portfolios can be part of the daily routine for students, as well.

Finally, how long do you add to and maintain the portfolio? Is it just for the academic year? If so, does it go home with the student at the end of the year? Is it cumulative? Does it go on to the next teacher? Is it evidence of your accountability? If so, does the school administrator keep it for evaluation purposes? The answers to these questions need to be addressed by each individual teacher within the local school setting.

The *how* of portfolio assessment is not unrelated to the *what* in the previous question. Jenny notes how important her interviews with the children are in completing the data collection. Mary Anne's letter home helps the parents understand her process. The parents in her class will not be seeing papers come home, as in the past. Both teachers recognize the structures they will need to modify in order to accomplish portfolio assessment.

Decision 5: What Decisions Can I Make from These Portfolios? When Is It a Portfolio?

First of all, when is it and when is it not a portfolio? Does a folder full of worksheets, teacher-made tests, and some observational data constitute a portfolio? The portfolio process should have all of the components identified in this chapter: activity dimensions (rationale, intentions, contents, standards, judgments), stakeholders, and historical dimensions. The criteria for evaluating the elements of the portfolio should consist of the following characteristics: Evidence of self-evaluation is apparent; the work is done *by* students instead of *to* them; traditional forms of assessment are appropriate if they fit

Jenny Cos

When questioned about the most important portfolio evidence, Jenny notes that the interviews with each child seem to be the most valuable source because she "tries to have the curriculum be as child-initiated as possible, incorporating the specific concept at the kindergarten level." She learns what they like straight from the children's mouths. Jenny's curriculum reflects this information. As one wanders around her classroom, it is clear that children have contributed to the curriculum planning.

Jenny related one emergent curriculum project that evolved out of some discussion among a small group of students about dinosaurs. The group expressed an interest in building a dinosaur. The group quickly became engaged in the project that involved planning, designing, choosing, constructing, directing, and engineering a model dinosaur. Jenny defined her role in this project as "passive observer." She collected the necessary materials and provided guidance when necessary. The learning she was able to document as a result of this activity was astounding: graphing, democratic process, scientific inquiry, problem solving, physics, and cooperative learning.

Mary Anne Davis

Mary Anne's letter to parents provides insight into the beginning *how, what,* and *why* of portfolios for this year's class.

Dear Parents:

We will be trying to collect portfolios this year in our room. I've been studying the concept for a couple of years and feel this is the time to give your children the opportunity to begin to evaluate their own work. Because we will be saving much of our work, you will not see much coming home. Please be patient with us, as this is a first attempt. We will begin immediately to save some "baseline" work with which to compare our progress. Also at this time, we will begin, as a group, to establish criteria for the pieces we save. I have set a number of pieces that must be saved in a special Showcase Portfolio. *The categories are: Most Important; Best Strategy; Most Growth; Worst; Worked on the Hardest; Like Best; and Process Pieces (all stages).*

To be continued...

---

with and enhance the process; and the contents should convey what the student has been doing, should be formative and summative, should inform instruction, may have multiple purposes, and should demonstrate progress.

If, in fact, you have an authentic portfolio, then you should be able to evaluate the contents and make the decisions that you intended to make. For instance, if you hope to assess the students for developmental capabilities, then the contents of the portfolio should provide authentic assessment of developmental status. Likewise, students who may be developmentally delayed or developmentally advanced should be identifiable via the portfolio evaluation.

Once the data are gathered, what do you do with it? Both Jenny and Mary Anne have just begun to wrestle with this question. Jenny knows she can modify curriculum plans by paying attention to what she sees collected in the portfolios. Mary Anne knows she wants to use the

---

Jenny Cos

With the dinosaur experience, as with any daily activity, Jenny sees the assessment process as ongoing. "You are assessing all the time by the activities you are doing in the group.... Why make every child who you know can do it go through the alphabet?... You can do it in a fun, informal way." Jenny described a cooperative group game called Ziparound that she uses to assess basic color and letter recognition, making anecdotal notes after the fact about her observations and using the information to focus children on skill building as they engage in other activities.

Parent Letter continued...

We will try to define what makes a piece "Most Important" or "The Hardest," and so on. It is necessary for the children to help set these standards so that they can begin to evaluate their own work. These portfolios are owned *by your child. They will decide what is saved and why. We will be respectful of these portfolios and their owners. I will view the work regularly* with *the children and you may also schedule a time to watch or review with us. I haven't set a time, as I have to wait and see when they are ready. Portfolios may* not *be viewed without your child and me present. I will also keep a teacher portfolio on each child with testing information and particular work that I need for grades.*

To be continued...

---

portfolios in an interactive way with parents rather than send the portfolio home without explanation. Still, little evidence is seen, so far, as to how the portfolios will fit into the "big picture."

Decision 6: How Do I Make the Portfolio Assessment Process an Ongoing, Consistent Process That Informs Curriculum and Instruction?

The portfolio assessment process, or any assessment process, needs to be an integral component in the curriculum planning and instructional process. In fact, there is a very logical loop that is formed when these functions become integral to the educational system. Curriculum is defined by a number of potential sources: professional association standards (e.g., National Council of Teachers of Mathematics [NCTM]), state curriculum models, local district courses of study, and the teacher's knowledge base. It is from the curriculum framework that a teacher plans the grade-level experiences. Assessment gives specific information about each child's development and abilities. Consequently, instructional strategies for teaching the curriculum may need to be modified in order to address individual student needs. Likewise, curriculum may also need to be modified or expanded, based on the assessment and instructional adjustments. The loop is begun and can continue throughout the academic year. Chapter 3 provides more specific examples of this feedback loop.

Both Jenny and Mary Anne give examples to think about how the portfolio assessment process fits into the curriculum-instruction-assessment feedback loop. The process is ongoing, it informs choices they make about curriculum and the types of instructional strategies they use, and it leads them back into the assessment process.

Jenny Cos

Jenny uses the portfolios for her parent conferences. She shares the contents as a way of documenting each child's progress over the semester and over the academic year. The contents are then the basis for discussing plans for the child and, at the end of the year, transition to the first grade. She finds that parents are usually more interested in discussing the transition in the final conference.

Jenny also uses the portfolio with the children as a way of revisiting their work for the year. They go over the portfolio together, "like a photo album and then they can take it home." For example, some of the observations that Jenny made during the dinosaur activity are shared with parents and pupils. She noted the following:

Use of democratic processes: voted to determine which dinosaur to build out of selections; the majority won

Mathematical concepts: measuring, counting, graphing, and problem solving

Cooperative learning: assignments of tasks/duties; someone recorded all decisions

Language development: celebration of creative expression, "verbal webbing" of ideas

Resource uses: used all areas of the classroom and resources to construct dinosaur

---

Mary Anne Davis

Parent Letter continued...

Children will keep unfinished work in their desks, finished work in an In Progress Portfolio, *and pieces that meet particular criteria for their own self-evaluation in the* Showcase Portfolio. *It is important to save many pieces in the* In Progress Portfolio *so that we have lots to choose from when looking for growth. Most children have no idea what makes their work "Great" or "Need Improvement." It is not enough anymore for me to evaluate them exclusively. They need to know, in no uncertain terms, how to assess their own learning and progress. I'll include our weekly notes on what we are doing with the portfolios. I truly believe that this is a great opportunity for all of us and, most of all, the children. I hope to include you shortly in our portfolio conferences. Be patient; we'll work as hard and as quickly as we can.*

Thank you for your patience,

Mary Anne Davis

IN CLOSING

Jenny Cos, Mary Anne Davis, and many other teachers have made the portfolio process an integral part of teaching practices. Jenny documents ongoing progress over time through a variety of methods: anecdotal records, interviews, children's self-assessment, parent information, and products. Mary Ann sees the process as dynamic and informative in terms of curriculum, instruction, and as a means of reporting progress. Both teachers have no doubt that this is the best method to document students' progress and inform curriculum.

Chapter 3

Design, Implementation, and Management

THINKING ABOUT IT
Mrs. Bain's Journal

9-24-96

Bingo! Sally did a neat in-service today where she had us tell her what we needed to learn about the authentic assessment/portfolio process so that we could get started in a small way. I guess I'm not alone in feeling unsure of how I'll get this done. So we decided, as a group, to start with the writing area first, since this is an area where the evidence is more obvious. But we started with the development of a rubric for assessing the quality of the writing samples. That was really helpful! I was surprised how clear in my mind my own standards for evaluating the kids' writing was. The things I learn about

---

*myself! So now I can start saving writing samples
and applying the rubric we came up with. I'm even
going to get the kids to choose a sample of their writing that they think is their best work and see if it
matches my standards.*

10-12-96

*Okay, so now I have all of these writing samples and
I've assessed them according to the criteria that we
established ... so what does all this tell me? Well, I
guess I can use them for the parent conferences coming up—and I was surprised that Tim, Jeanna, and
Will are having such a hard time with the continuity
of their writing. I need to work with them on this—
maybe in a small group while the other kids are
going about their business. Good idea!*

10-20-96

*The small group work has given me more informa-
tion about these kids than I ever imagined. I tried it
first with the three who were having such difficulty
on the continuity component. They each read their
writing to the group and the group helped them evaluate whether there was a continuous story line, with
my guidance, of course. I was amazed at how good
they were at picking up on the problems each seemed
to be having. All three were able to revise their stories*

and the results were outstanding! Who would ever
have thought that they could be so helpful to each
other? This portfolio stuff is more than just assessment; I think it may actually change the way I try to
teach writing. Hmmm, small groups, peer
critique…it has possibilities maybe in the other content areas!!!

10-23-96

Okay…I think I have the writing portion of the portfolio under control. The kids are choosing representative products to put in the portfolio and we are jointly
evaluating their progress and setting some short-
term goals. Darrell and I sat together yesterday and
talked about his writing samples in the portfolio. I
was surprised that he chose one that was not really
his best work. In fact, the thing was laced with my
comments, and his peer reviewers were even less
kind. He told me that he put that piece in the portfolio so that he would remember the skills he needed to
work on. Well, he was right, and we used that paper
to set his goals. I would never have chosen that example to put in for posterity, but for him, it was a clear
guideline. I suppose if I write an anecdotal note
about that and attach it to the sample, it will be clear
to all who "enter" his portfolio. I'll make a note to
myself to do this…

In discussions with teachers who use portfolio assessment models, three issues are raised time and again: design, implementation, and management. How do you design a portfolio assessment system? How do you find the time to implement a portfolio assessment system? How do you manage it once you do?

Although it is true that good teachers find time for things that are important, it is also true that the school day is increasingly hectic with a feeling that there is little or no time to add something "new." One of the advantages of using a portfolio assessment system is that it should be designed to help you capitalize on those things that you are already doing. In fact, other teachers who have used portfolio models for several years have commented on the fact that, although it does take a bit to get organized, once that is complete, they actually have additional time to spend with students. Additionally, portfolio assessment is not designed to be the sole responsibility of the teacher; it is a joint effort between student/teacher/parent/community members. Therefore, as appropriate for the age/grade of the student, teachers relinquish responsibility for management to the student. This chapter will examine design issues and then look at teacher practices that support the implementation and management of the portfolio assessment system.

In reviewing the description of Kathy's classroom, note that her first consideration was the linkage between curriculum, instruction, and assessment. In reflecting on her philosophy as a teacher, she began to realize that there was a discrepancy between and among the critical elements of her classroom. She began to look for a means

Kathy Montague—Sixth Grade

Kathy Montague teaches sixth-grade students in a suburban school. Over the last several years, she has augmented her assessment of students with a portfolio-based process. After many years of teaching, she felt the need to employ strategies for reporting students' progress that were more parallel with her instructional philosophy and practices. Kathy's curriculum and instructional practices had evolved into what might be described as constructivist in nature. Her strategies were designed to engage the students in manipulation, exploration, and investigation of materials within the classroom. With feedback from the environment (e.g., teacher, materials, peers), students were guided in constructing new knowledge from these experiences. Kathy felt that traditional forms of assessment were not supplying her with the whole picture of what her students could do, what they had tried to accomplish, and their level of self-direction; nor did they reinforce her view of instruction. Kathy started out her search for a "better" way to assess writing.

that would provide a more accurate picture of her students' learning. You can also see that Kathy did not begin with the entire curriculum. She began with a simple question: How can I more accurately represent the students' writing development in this classroom?

DESIGNING A PORTFOLIO SYSTEM

Chapter 2 explained that teachers need to make a series of decisions about the portfolio assessment system that they wish to employ. Looking at areas to assess—which may include cognitive, affective, and physical develop-

AT A GLANCE...
Designing a Portfolio Plan

◆ Determine the criteria and/or standards to become the framework for the portfolio assessment system.

◆ Translate the criteria and/or standards into observable behaviors.

◆ Using the criteria, examine the scope and sequence of the curriculum to determine an approximate time frame for collecting evidence and completing evaluations.

◆ Determine the stakeholders in the portfolio model.

◆ Determine the types of evidence to be collected.

◆ Determine a method by which evidence will be transformed into decision making.

◆ Establish a system for conferencing and reporting assessment information and decisions.

◆ Establish a series of exemplary pieces/portfolios by age/grade/content to provide a comparison.

ment—are preliminary decisions to the design itself. Once the area(s) have been established, then teachers need to create a structure for the assessment portfolio. Several critical steps should be included in the design process

As already noted, a portfolio assessment model can encompass a wide array of student skills, attitudes, and development. In order to look more closely at the structure of a portfolio assessment model, consider the assessment of exceptional potential or giftedness in young children. The *Early Assessment for Exceptional Potential (EAEP)* model (Shaklee et al., 1990) was designed to be used in primary classrooms in order to identify areas of potential or talent in young minority children.

Establishing Criteria or Standards for Assessment

Following the eight guidelines, the first step in the process for the EAEP program was to establish the criteria or standards by which the assessment would take place. In order to determine the criteria, we turned to the research literature on young gifted minority students and found a list of attributes or primary identifiers that were evident in many of these students. However, a list of attributes is insufficient for our purposes because each teacher or adult involved with students would define the attribute differently and we wanted to assess students consistently. For example, if an attribute said "Exceptional Memory," we would ask how that would look in a first-grade classroom, in a second-grade classroom, in a third-grade classroom, and so on. Taking those same attributes and establishing a list of examples of how that might look in the classroom improves one's ability to accurately observe this identifier. In the case of EAEP, the primary identifiers and subsequent examples looked like this:

Exceptional Learner

Attribute	*Example*
Exceptional Memory	From a kindergartner: "Mercury is the planet closest to the sun and it's hot on one side and cold on the other and it's small and it's named after a god."
	From a first-grader: "The name of that thing that we used last year to look at rocks was a microscope."

The same process would be true if a teacher decided to assess affective development, content knowledge, and skill in mathematics or literacy development. In each area, establishing the criteria or standards for assessment would provide the framework for the remainder of the assessment design.

The second step is to assure that the criteria or standards are observable and appropriate to the age/grade/content areas of the students to be assessed. Although the EAEP model focused on the research literature about gifted minority students, Kathy Montague, as an individual teacher, drew from a different knowledge base.

Kathy Montague

Kathy started out her search for a way to assess children's progress by trying to create a rubric to guide her evaluation of the writing process. She sought literature to guide and affirm her ideas about the rubric she was creating. Authors such as Reggie Routman, Donald Graves, Lucy Caulkins, and Ken Goodman provided her with a solid base for pursuing the writing rubric. Once she felt comfortable with the clarity and directness of the criteria, Kathy gave the rubric to the students so that they could keep track of their writing progress and so they could share their progress with their parents. The strategy proved most useful and seemed to be a good fit with her notion of best instructional practice. It was not long before she expanded the process, making it a multipurpose portfolio covering a number of content areas.

Note that as Kathy had an opportunity to work with a small part of the curriculum using portfolio assessment, she began to see additional ways to expand the portfolio process. She realized that she could manage this process and wanted to add other areas of the curriculum. She selected reading, writing, and mathematics. In addition, she wanted to establish ownership and responsibility on the part of the students for elements of the portfolio process. Finally, she realized that she wanted parents to have a stake in the portfolio assessment process, as well. Conducting portfolio assessment is a learning process for the teacher, too. Expansion of the portfolio is a natural outgrowth once the management issues have been mastered.

Stakeholders and Sources of Evidence

Stakeholders and sources of evidence are often combined in the actual planning of portfolio models because it is easier to think about what kind of information is wanted at the same time that you are thinking about who you want it from. In many new portfolio assessment systems, it is not unusual to find only two stakeholders: the teacher and the student. Ultimately, however, in order to provide for a broader and more credible picture of the student's development, other stakeholders should be included in the process. Most teachers add the class-mates next, through surveys or peer editing/review activities, then resource teachers, and, finally, the parents.

In the EAEP program, a decision was made that parents/community members, regular classroom teachers, students, and resource specialists were people who might have important information about these young children. Once that decision was made, we began a process of determining how we could collect accurate information from them and in what manner. In the case of parent/community members, we adapted a survey from Delisle (1990) and distributed a *Home / Community Survey* to all students in the class (see Figure 3–1). The "glue" for the survey was our original primary identifiers with each question related to one of the attributes of exceptional potential.

	Quite Often	Sometimes	Seldom	Comments
1. My child often remembers things and can give a lot of detail about the situation.				
2. My child continues to work on a project even when faced with temporary setbacks or slow progress.				
3. My child suggests imaginative ways of doing things, even if the suggestions are sometimes impractical.				

FIGURE 3–1   *Home / Community Survey*

Source: Adapted from "Things My Child Likes to Do" in *Guiding the Social and Emotional Development of Gifted Youth* by J. Delisle, 1992, New York: Longman.

By asking parents and community members to provide a specific example of the identifier, we could check for understanding as well as gather other information about home activities. A similar structure was used to collect student/self-information regarding attributes of exceptional potential. In this case, we constructed a device called *Who Do You Know?* Using primary identifiers as criteria, we asked students to identify other students or themselves as possessing a particular attribute. Questions such as "Who do you know who has a good memory?" or "Who do you know who tells the best stories with words and actions?" allowed students to contribute information to the portfolio assessment process.

The portfolio contents included materials that Kathy had gleaned from her own ideas about portfolio assess-

Kathy Montague

Once the commitment to portfolio assessment was made, Kathy had a number of decisions to make in order to implement her plan. First, she needed to determine who her stakeholders were. She, of course, was the obvious stakeholder. Her plan to make the students more responsible in the process certainly tagged them as critical stakeholders. By viewing the students as members of the assessment team, Kathy removed the air of secrecy often surrounding the assessment process (Wiggins, 1993). Kathy also identified the parents as important partners in the assessment team. Kathy then turned her focus to what kinds and types of evidence she wanted to collect. "Trying to think of authentic pieces of evidence to put in the portfolio in order to demonstrate progress in writing was easy. Math was a harder one. I try to use real-life applications of math for this. Like I ask them to make muffins for 4 people using a recipe designed for 25 people. If they can do this, then they have successfully used fractions and I can record that experience."

ment and materials she found in a resource on student-led conferences called *Together Is Better* (Davies, Cameron, Politano, & Gregory, 1992). Sometimes, Kathy had to be creative in the way in which she thought about evidence collection. Typically, one thinks of written products because they are the primary product of most school days. By expanding her repertoire to include observations, pictures, and recordings, Kathy has been able to capture learning from a variety of different dimensions.

Establishing a Timeline

Another step in beginning to implement a portfolio process is to establish a tentative timeline. What information will be collected and when it will be collected should be embedded into your day-to-day planning of lessons. Using the identified criteria, examine the scope and sequence of the curriculum to determine a schedule for data collection and evaluation of the data for decision making. For example, Mr. Wainwright decided that in addition to student-selected samples of writing, he wanted to make a selection from each student once a month. On his lesson plan book, he notes the date and reminds himself to collect all student writing samples for the portfolio. Another teacher, Mrs. Alexander, in an effort to collect anecdotal notes about her students, has established a classroom chart using pull-off labels (see Figure 3–2).

As you can see from Figure 3–2, Mrs. Alexander lists each student in the class and a series of projected weeks in which she wants to be *sure* to collect an anecdotal record on each child. She may have additional anecdotal notes that she will collect during this period, but she uses this method as a prompt to remember to observe each child carefully during mathematics. As Mrs. Alexander noted, "When I first started using anecdotal notes, I

Sara Jones	9/26 good focus during problem-solving group	10/3 some difficulty with understanding decimals
Mike McCardy	9/26 tried three different solutions to the problem	10/3 persistent; helped Albert with math
Josie Jenks	9/26 worked independently	10/3 peer edited with Mike; good understanding
Albert Anderson	9/26 demonstrated to other students	10/3 independent work at learning center; well done
Bill Sharpless	9/26 solved problem independently; much effort	10/3 completed math portfolio for the week; on task

FIGURE 3–2 *Math Observations*

found that there were some kids I just couldn't write about. My attention was often turned to those who seemed to demand it; I had a lot of notes on them. In order to help me focus and to find out about those 'missing' children, I created a plan for note taking. Now, if a student's note isn't removed from the chart, I know I haven't looked closely at [that child] this week. The students know it too—in fact, some of the kids are asking if I will be writing about them this week."

Further, Mrs. Alexander made the decision to collect only "strength" notes. She spoke about this way: "We often take notes on what students can't do, what they don't achieve, or how poorly they behave. We seldom take notes on what children do well, what they can achieve, and when they are exhibiting age-appropriate behaviors. I want to see my students in a positive light, I want them to see what they can achieve, so I take strength notes."

We talked with Mrs. Alexander further, wanting to know if she ignores the inappropriate behavior or lack of achievement. She noted, "Absolutely not, but you know what I have found out? I can tell by what I am writing what a student has been doing. For instance, when I write that Janet was 'focused on her work for 10 minutes,' one day and the next 'focused for 30 minutes,' I know that Janet has a hard time staying on task and is increasing her ability to do so. I don't have to write a negative note to find that out." Mrs. Alexander has long observed students' behavior. Every teacher does. What the process of portfolio assessment is designed to do is to help Mrs. Alexander focus her observations, create a way to make sense of those observations, and use them along with other pieces of data to make decisions for her class.

At the beginning of the design process, think about what you already do and when you do it. If it is a natural part of your practice to make observations of student progress, work on how to write your observations down and where they should go (e.g., teacher portfolio or student portfolio). Remember, you may want to take notes on everything, but the focus of anecdotal note taking should be directly related to the framework for your portfolio effort. Notes that document progress, thinking, and actions in mathematics, for instance, or anecdotes that target literacy activities are all valuable forms of evidence.

Finally, in crafting a timeline for evidence collection as an individual teacher, note it in your planning book. You will be less likely to forget if you see the comment "Collect math samples." If you are working with a larger group (e.g., team or schoolwide), you may wish to establish a common timeline for evidence collection. The advantage of a common timeline is that you can look within your class and across classes at student growth and development if all teachers make similar selections at the same time (e.g., a spontaneous writing sample from every student at the beginning of the year). A schoolwide timeline might look something like Figure 3–3.

Note in the schoolwide timeline not all evidence is collected throughout the year. The decision of when to collect certain pieces of evidence is based on several issues: timeliness, congruence with the curriculum, and student development. Clearly, some pieces are more appropriately collected at one time versus another. Initial parent information should be collected early in the year to provide an avenue of conversation and to let parents know that you are interested in their child's development. Another issue is congruence with the curriculum. When, in the normal course of the year, do certain events happen? In an effort to collect evidence from activities that are meaningful for the student, look for events, activities, and opportunities for students to engage in authentic learning. For example, writing samples from reflections on a trip to NASA Space Center will be more likely to produce authentic responses than a teacher prompt of "Write about going into space."

Finally, when creating a timeline, think about student development. For instance, one teacher noted that asking for a peer nomination from students would be most appropriate some time in October or November, after the students have had ample opportunity to get to

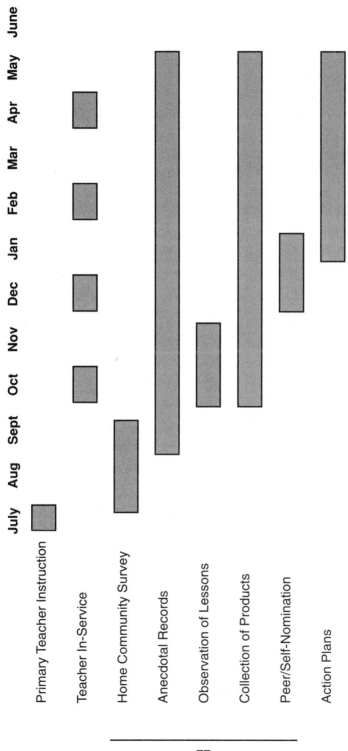

FIGURE 3-3 *EAEP Timeline*

know one another, not at the beginning of the year when they are getting acquainted.

Collecting Evidence

Teachers and students have long collected student work in a folder, pizza box, mailbox, or notebook of some sort. The difference between a collection of student work and a portfolio is that every piece of work that is in a portfolio is there for a *specific* reason. The work represents growth toward, or recognition of, a particular goal. This also means that the work in the portfolio is limited; it is not the sum total of all the work that a student has completed during the course of a year. Rather, it is a representative sample selected to demonstrate growth and achievement in a particular dimension of learning (e.g., mathematics, literacy, science, etc.).

Some teachers choose to keep two portfolios on each student. One is a working portfolio in which the student keeps all of his or her work. Once a week or every two weeks, students and the teacher review the working portfolio and select specific pieces of work to move into the assessment portfolio. The assessment portfolio includes pieces of work that demonstrate development and those that demonstrate "best" work for that student based on the framework of the portfolio.

Working through student choices and decisions can have a humorous side. When working with third-graders, Mrs. Adams noticed that the students would select only those papers that she had already graded or corrected, not what they really thought was their best effort, thus, defeating the purpose of student selection. She decided that each student would have to choose before she reviewed the work: "I got worried about what parents would think if they saw work that wasn't reviewed or corrected. I didn't know what to do. Finally, I decided that each piece of evidence within the portfolio would be marked T, S, or P—that is, T for teacher choice, S for student choice, and P for parent choice. That way, parents would always know who made the selection for the portfolio and why it may not have been corrected by me."

This strategy has worked effectively for Mrs. Adams, but it may not be for you. Each teacher needs to decide what he or she is comfortable with, what fits his or her practice, and what they can live with in the classroom. If the idea of two portfolios on every student seems overwhelming, then start with one. If asking parents to contribute to the portfolio is perplexing to you, then do not begin with that element. Select those elements of evidence collection that best fit your practice, try them out until you and your students feel comfortable, and then begin to expand the portfolio assessment process.

It is clear when you look at these materials that Kathy has shared the responsibility for assessing with her students and has placed the responsibility for reporting progress in the hands of her students. Kathy describes her experiences with the portfolio assessment process as rewarding. She is constantly impressed with the self-sufficiency, poise, and ownership demonstrated by her students. "Students are learning to be responsible for themselves, their behavior. If a student hasn't reached his or her goal, [he or she receives] specific feed-

Kathy Montague

Kathy made two decisions that modified her classroom environment. First, she decided to develop a portfolio for each student in order to keep an ongoing record of academic progress. Second, she decided to make all students responsible for setting goals, recording accomplishments, and reporting their progress to their parents. Using her earlier resources, Kathy established three packets of information: Goal-Setting Conference; Informal Communication; and Conference Notes. Included in each packet of information was a timeline for the goal-setting conference, a schedule of telephone contacts, written forms for parents requesting additional input, and the timeline for the semi-annual three-way conferences.

back from the parent/teacher team. [The student then rewrites his or her] goals for the upcoming semester. This self-evaluation is more powerful than a report card. I try to help them be successful."

Transforming Evidence into Decisions

One of the most difficult areas of transition in portfolio assessment is taking the information that has been collected in the portfolio and using it for decision making on behalf of students. Perhaps a reason for this difficulty is the design of the portfolios themselves. They often focus on collecting student products according to specific standards but they do not include a method by which that information is used in planning and instruction. Chapter 4 focuses more specifically on curriculum and instructional practices, but this section discusses how teachers view the evidence within the portfolio and how they begin to make curricular decisions.

When you begin collecting specific evidence that relates directly to the criteria you are trying to assess, you may find it overwhelming to think about going through all of the materials in each student's portfolio when you have 30 students in your class. One method that may assist you is to create some sort of process that will allow you to combine the evidence for a quick look, knowing that you can always go back for more specific information within the portfolio as needed. A method that we have used includes a variety of simple forms that teachers could use to look across the class without having to look at individual folders. For example, when completing a series of observations on students across six or seven different lessons, you could construct a form that resembles Figure 3–4.

By color coding each of the observations you make during problem-solving activities, you can quickly note which students understand and can follow the steps in problem solving as well as where students are experiencing difficulties. Instead of looking through each individual portfolio, you will have an across-the-class look at problem solving at your fingertips.

Another strategy to employ is to combine information from specific products as well as observations within a

Class Names	Identifies Facts	Identifies Problem	Employs 5-Step Process	Proposes and Evaluates Solution
John Jacobs				
Marissa Smith				
Tanya Sorento				
Juan Cortez				

FIGURE 3–4 *Observations in Problem Solving*

portfolio to describe the evidence within the portfolio. In this case, completed individually, a teacher can again look quickly at the evidence without having to look at each piece within the portfolio. In the EAEP project, our teachers used a form for each individual child to look at products and observations (see Figure 3–5). As teachers and students collected evidence in the portfolio, a note was made on the form regarding the fact that the portfolio held a product that provided evidence of exceptional learning and/or the teacher had made observations of exceptionality during a specific learning opportunity.

Systems for Conference and Reporting

The strategies employed for reporting information from the portfolio are varied according to the age of the students and the level of involvement of the parents as well as the time restrictions on conferencing and reporting at the local level. At the most simple level, teachers use the portfolio as a means to provide parents with direct information and evidence of their child's performance. Much in the same way student work was shared in the past, the portfolio contents are used to highlight strengths and weaknesses during a specific period of time. At the most complex level, the portfolio is used as a means to assist the student, parent, and teacher to provide feedback, determine strengths and weaknesses, and determine new goals. As seen earlier, Kathy Montague has established a systematic method to promote student-led conferences. As her students begin to prepare for their semi-annual conference, they each spend time working on "Student's Notes" (see Figure 3–6).

Kathy's system is more complex, in part because her students are older and because she enjoys the support of the parents. The parents have come to expect their child to be able to articulate learning goals, to make an accurate assessment of their progress, and to establish new goals as the year progresses. Kathy is not only helping her sixth-graders become more self-directed but she is also helping them become life-long learners. Further, with the parents' support, she is helping her sixth-graders accept responsibility for their learning.

Collecting Exemplars

A final element in portfolio design is to begin a collection of exemplars of student work across grade levels and within content areas. For example, select and copy examples of student writing for fifth-graders that is age appropriate, developmentally delayed, or developmentally

Performance Assessment

Lessons	Exceptional Learner	
	Products	Observations
1.		
2.		
3.		
4.		
5.		
6.		
1. Additional Samples of Products (C) (T) (H)		
2.		
3.		
4.		
5.		

FIGURE 3–5 *Evaluation of Portfolio Contents (Products and Observations)*

Student Name _____

Exceptional User of Knowledge		Exceptional Generator of Knowledge		Exceptional Motivation	
Products	Observations	Products	Observations	Products	Observations

Funded by U.S. Department of Education, Grant No. R206A00160
Property of Early Assessment for Exceptional Potential Grant

Conference #_____

Student's Notes—Reading

(Welcome everyone to the conference. Say something about *why* we are all here today.)

First, I would like to discuss my strengths, and areas for improvement in reading.

These are the things I am really good at in reading:_____

Here's why I think I am good at these things (show your proof):

_____

I think I need to spend more time on: _____

because (show your proof): _____

Now I would like to demonstrate some of my reading skills for you by playing a tape of myself reading. I chose this piece because:

_____

Now is also a good time to discuss my reading goals (state your goals): _____

FIGURE 3–6 *Student Conference Plan*

advanced. The collection is used in two ways. First, it serves as a comparison for teachers and students as they compare work samples to a selected standard and decide on new student goals. Second, the collection can be used during teacher/parent conferences to provide the parent with a frame of reference. What do most fifth-graders do in writing? What is an acceptable standard? What is advanced writing for fifth graders? Further, the collection can be used to help new teachers understand the portfolio assessment system and develop a frame of reference for his or her own class.

IN CLOSING

Portfolio assessment evidence is similar to the types of evidence that teachers have been using for a long time: pupil products, anecdotal records, observations, tests/quizzes, student self-reports/surveys, student conferences, and so on. Probably the only source of information that teachers have not traditionally and systematically collected is information from parents and community members regarding student interests and learning. Portfolio assessment is designed to help you make the best use of all the information you already have at your disposal, to be able to make more precise decisions based on a broad collection of evidence.

Teachers must also ask the question: What am I giving up? Unlikely as this may seem, when you implement a well-designed portfolio assessment system, it should take the place of some of the traditional methods you have been using. Your design for assessment will encompass a much broader array of pieces of evidence than traditionally used in the classroom. One of our teachers put it this way: "When I first began using a portfolio assessment system, it was an addition—a burden on top of everything else I was doing. Then I began to see where it fit, how it became part of my practice. For example, I stopped doing chapter tests in one unit because all of the other evidence accounted for all of the skills that were part of the chapter test. It wasn't necessary."

Seeing what can be replaced and moving ahead with those decisions takes time. Most teachers—including Jenny, Mary Anne, and Kathy—see portfolio assessment as an ongoing process, gradually shaping their practice.

Chapter 4

Using Portfolio Results in Planning Instruction

THINKING ABOUT IT

Mrs. Bain's Journal

11-15-96

So now I want to do the same "rubric development" with the reading area that we did with the writing. I talked with two of my grade-level colleagues and we decided to get together and brainstorm a similar kind of rubric for reading. It was a little harder to do this because things like comprehension are tough to define in terms of behavior. So we just started listing the things we noticed about kids who were comprehending the stories we read. It was a snap from there. I CAN do this if I keep it simple.

11-30-96

The rubric for comprehension seems to be working. I can better document who is reading AND understanding the story. Mostly, I have been able to see how boring the typical questions have been. I have some more natural methods of determining the students' comprehension by opening up my way of assessing it. And the other parts come along for the ride! Like, just from listening to the kids relate the content of the story to their own lives, they are using the new vocabulary from the story, so I know that they have problem solved definitions and context from their reading activity. Or maybe I'm just listening differently ....

12-10-96

Math, math math—now we're working on the math portfolio component. I know what our goals are for math, but I'm trying hard to think of ways for the kids to demonstrate their competency in this area so that it's like the writing and reading part—not just test scores—something more. I need to think this one through; observe them as they do the math activities. ...HELP!!!

Embedded in a portfolio assessment approach are questions that relate to curriculum, instructional practices, and the use of information in a timely and effective manner. The purpose of this chapter is to discuss and provide examples of curriculum adaptations that you might want to consider given the evidence collected within a portfolio.

As we have worked with teachers on portfolio assessment, we have identified some common concerns as well as surprises. The original concerns expressed were: Would teachers really do all of the design work involved in constructing a portfolio model? and Would teachers (and students) be able to manage all of the data collection? Fortunately, in our case and in many others, the answer was a resounding yes! Teachers and students were most willing to design and implement a portfolio assessment system. What we found very surprising was that making the transition from collecting information to *using the information to make curricular or instructional decisions on behalf of children was a struggle.* In part, this was due to lack of a planning process. It became clear, however, that teachers often relied on an intuitive sense rather than a systematic process to make decisions and to determine whether a curricular change was effective. In one classroom, the process went something like this:

Mr. Tanagelo had conducted portfolio assessments in mathematics beginning in September with 24 fourth-grade students. His portfolio design was based on five levels of math proficiency: concrete learner, applied learner, analytic learner, symbolic learner, and authentic learner. In each category, using NCTM guidelines, he had described and defined the indicators of when a child was functioning at that level in mathematics instruction. Further, he was systematically collecting and evaluating the following evidence for each child in the class: anecdotal records, student self-evaluations, checklists, learning logs, quizzes and tests, and student products. This process allowed Mr. Tanagelo to identify and provide instruction to children according to the continuum of levels of mathematical proficiency.

During a discussion, Mr. Tanagelo was asked to explain how he used this information not only to confirm a student's level of math proficiency but also to structure the environment to give the student an opportunity to gain the skills and understandings necessary to move to the next level. He replied, "Well, I provide a lot of opportunities across the continuum of levels for students to engage in math learning." Probing a bit further, we asked, "But how do you *know* that what you are providing is congruent with what *a* specific child might need to grow and learn?" Thinking quietly, he said, "You know, I don't think I can answer that. I think that is what has been bothering me but I didn't know it. I collect all of this information—kids love it, parents love it, and I really do know more about my students than in the past—but I don't really use it to change what *I* do."

This is the heart of the discussion on portfolio assessment—to use what you know to benefit the child. When and how the teacher makes decisions, implements changes, and *evaluates those changes for effectiveness* determines how well he or she uses the information collected about students. The teacher is in the process of refining what he or she knows about children, teaching, curriculum, instruction, and assessment. It is this delicate balance of identifying what children know and how they learn, matched with curriculum and instructional practices, continually informed by assessment that the teacher is trying to achieve. One piece without the others is virtually useless. This chapter will highlight some specific examples of teachers and students using portfolio assessment information to inform instruction.

CURRICULUM

As you may recall, thematic or interdisciplinary approaches to curriculum coupled with an active learning environment appear to support portfolio assessment models. The selection of curriculum should reflect the underlying principles of the discipline itself (e.g., what does a historian do to study history?) as well as the standards, goals, or objectives designed by the district/state or nationally recognized organization (e.g., NAEYC, National Council of Teachers of Mathematics). Beyond the adoption of a general curricula for all students comes specific curriculum selected by a teacher or a team of teachers (e.g., most second-graders study the community while many sixth-graders study state history). It is within those specific areas that teachers make decisions about what to offer and how to offer it to students. It is also at this juncture that teachers should be making decisions using portfolio evidence about what areas and which techniques could best foster growth and development for a student. Additionally, it is at this point that differentiated curriculum may be used to reach the same or similar goals for all students.

INSIDE A PRIMARY CLASSROOM

The primary team at a local elementary school has been working on differentiated curriculum for the past several years. The team meets once a week for an extended planning period. At that time, issues, concerns, and future plans are discussed.

In this session, teachers are talking about the upcoming study of the local community. As in everything they do, all children (including those with special needs) participate in the unit. The decisions being made today are directly related to the portfolio assessment data that have been collected on each child. The first round of discussion is to decide which activities will be done with the whole group—guest speakers (mayor, fire chief, and police chief), a walking tour around the community, group brainstorming on topics of student interest, and group activities related to certain key principles (e.g., what makes a community), to name a few. The second round of decisions are based on the student-generated list of interests in government, businesses, transportation, and entertainment (see Figure 4–1).

At this juncture, teachers matched students (from portfolio evidence) with specific areas of interests and

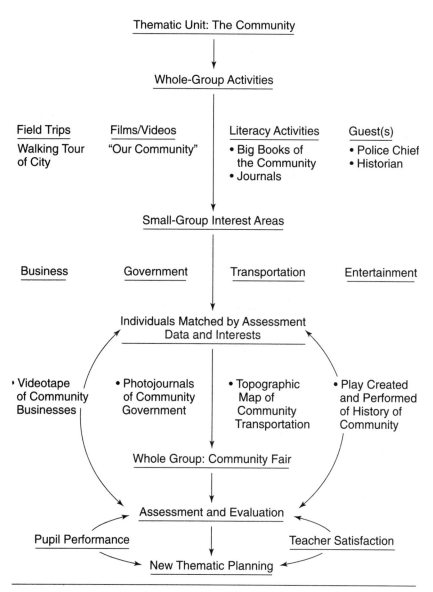

FIGURE 4–1 *Thematic Unit*

tasks. For example, children exhibiting a preference for a visual style of learning are assigned to make a videotape of the community; other children will interview key persons (e.g., the Director of Parks and Recreation); and still others will build a topographic map of the community. In each case, students will be given an opportunity to share what they learned about their community with other students and teachers. In addition, each child will complete a self-evaluation of his or her work as well as a conference with the teacher on this aspect of the community project for his or her portfolio.

To assist them with their planning, the primary teachers used a Curriculum Action Planner. The planner identifies who is in need of specific learning opportunities, what activities/resources students will be engaged in, any additional resources needed, and the means of evaluation. Although teachers often use traditional planning devices, the purpose of using the Curriculum Action Planner is to tie the portfolio evidence more closely to the instructional plan (see Figure 4–2).

Finally, the primary team established several evaluation questions to be answered and determined what evidence would be collected at the close of the unit that related to both student performance and teacher satisfaction. Among the questions asked were:

How well did students learn the concepts of community?

How well did students perform within the small-group assignments?

Teacher(s): _____ Grade: _____ Date: _____

Changes/Adaptations in Curriculum for:

Alternatives to Provide:

___ Learning   ___ Enrichment   ___ Remediation
    Centers   Materials

___ Curriculum   ___ Extension Lessons ___ Contracts
    Compactor

___ Creative   ___ Critical Thinking ___ Small Group
    Thinking

___ Thematic Unit   ___ Individualized in _____

Resources Needed (materials/people):

Phase One: Action Plan (who and what):

Timeline:

Assessment and Evaluation:

___

FIGURE 4–2 *Curriculum Action Planner*

How did the team like the large-group and small-group structure?

What changes would the team make before teaching this unit again?

Evidence for decision making was collected through formal and informal observations, student tests, pupil products evaluated on specific criteria, and pupil/teacher conferences. The results of these questions are used to plan future activities, monitor student progress, and determine to what degree the plan, based on evidence within the student portfolio, was effective. Evident in the primary team's planning is the cycle of Curriculum–Instruction–Assessment, which leads to a new C–I–A cycle based on the systematic examination of student progress and teacher satisfaction. It is this ongoing dynamic that makes meaningful use of information collected in student portfolios. In order to provide for the variety of student learning needs identified through portfolio assessment, teachers not only examined differentiated curriculum but also identified differentiated instructional strategies to complement student learning.

INSTRUCTIONAL STRATEGIES

In looking for instructional strategies, teachers must be on a constant search for what processes and content can be used to allow students to maximize their learning. Differentiated instructional opportunities range from types and levels of questions asked of students to instruction based on learning centers to allowing students to proceed with their work through an independent study. The key is to match the instructional techniques with student skills and strengths to maximize the learning process.

In addition to the match, teachers must carefully and systematically evaluate the impact of the match to ensure student development in all areas—cognitive, affective, and physical. The NAEYC position statement on developmentally appropriate practice would view this process as the *precision* it takes not only to establish an age-appropriate classroom but also to attend to the inter-/intraindividual differences that each child brings to school. A brief discussion on several options for differentiation is presented next.

Thinking Skills/Models

Educators have long recognized the benefit of asking students a broad array of questions that foster critical thinking skills. Teaching strategies include a variety of models from direct instruction (Beyer, 1991) to Socratic discussions (Paul, 1991) to fostering creative thinking through questioning (Perkins, 1991). Further, McTighe and Lyman (1991) suggest that thinking can be cued by using a series of specific strategies that foster the link between the process to be used and the way in which the concept is best learned. For example, the Think-Pair-Share process, which is a "multi-mode discussion cycle in which students listen to a question or presentation, have time to think individually, talk with each other in pairs, and finally share with the larger group" (p. 243) can be used as a specific strategy to help students develop thinking skills.

Although it is important that all children have the benefit of learning specific thinking strategies, it is also important that once learned, students have a responsibility to selectively use those strategies that match the content, process, and their own individual learning needs. It is, at this point, that teachers can help students by differentiating the instructional process used based on portfolio evidence.

Looking at whole-language instruction will offer a view of this process. According to McTighe and Lyman (1991), certain strategies are used by good readers. These include concentration, monitoring, and flexibility. Poor readers typically do not have those skills and view reading as a discrete process rather than a whole. The *Ready Reading Reference* bookmark was created by Kapinus (1986) and is used to guide poor readers during the reading process. The bookmark uses questions and processes for both the teacher and the student, such as utilizing Think-Pair-Share, asking follow-up questions, asking higher-level questions, or providing for student summaries of information.

Based on evidence collected within the portfolio, a teacher might choose to provide bookmarks to those readers who need additional support and to focus some specific instructional time with those readers. Is this to say that the teacher ignores or does not provide for good readers? No; the teacher tries to refine the process of instruction based on specific evidence found in the reading portfolio. The teacher does not assume that because it is good for one child, it is good for all; rather, the teacher makes sure that he or she has a "good fit" to maximize student learning. In this balance, one recognizes that children should not spend time learning things they already know (which is evidenced in the portfolio). Instead, students should spend time in new learning and growth. One of the best references on thinking skills and questioning strategies is *Developing Minds* (Costa, 1991), published by Association for Supervision and Curriculum Development.

Replacement: Extension, Acceleration, Remediation

Another decision that can be made is to replace assignments or content based on evidence found within a portfolio. For example, when Susan demonstrated her skill in mathematics (e.g., two-digit multiplication), Mr. Wainwright knew that she no longer needed to work through that section of math. Additionally, looking at other portfolios of students' work, Mr. Wainwright found several others who also had acquired these skills. At this point, Mr. Wainwright had a decision to make: extension or acceleration?

Depending on the evidence within the math portfolio, Mr. Wainwright may decide to accelerate Susan's math instruction based on additional assessment data (e.g., chapter tests or end-of-year tests) or he could decide that although Susan does not need to continue with these particular math experiences, she would benefit by extension lessons. In this instance, Mr. Wainwright decided to provide a mathematics center that required students to extend their math skills by creating a flight plan for a trip from Washington, DC, to Moscow, Russia. During direct instruction in math, Susan and her cohorts work at the math center.

At the same time that Mr. Wainwright has identified learning strengths for Susan and others, he has also identified, through evidence collected in portfolios, some students who need additional work on multiplication. In this instance, Mr. Wainwright decides to engage these students in cooperative learning activities that emphasize the successful use of multiplication strategies to solve a mathematical mystery story. Mr. Wainwright continues to collect information through student products and anecdotal records in order to evaluate the impact of the alternative activities on each student's understanding and skills in the use of multiplication.

Independent Study/Individualized Projects

In a few instances, teachers may find that a student needs an individualized or independent program for part of the day. Again, the evidence to indicate this need is derived directly from the portfolio. Using a multiage approach to instruction, Mrs. Flarida found that she had a wide continuum of reading skills and abilities within her classroom. Although she focused her efforts using a whole-language approach, she found that a few students needed help with decoding skills and a few others were fluent readers. Mrs. Flarida even had one student who was an accelerated reader, far beyond the rest of the class.

In order to accommodate the wide variety within the class, Mrs. Flarida selected a thematic unit on inventors/inventions as her focal point. With inventors as a starting point, she collected a variety of tradebooks that ranged from simple to highly complex. For example, she had books on Einstein that typically would have been categorized as primary through precollegiate level. When students selected their inventor to study, she guided (not limited) their selection of resources according to her reading indicators in the portfolio: emergent, developing, or fluent. She also considered work habits and evidence of self-directed learning that she had collected through observations and anecdotal records. Using this information, Mrs. Flarida structured the class in a manner that would allow students to move through the unit in small groups or independently.

At each decision-making point, Mrs. Flarida considers carefully which individuals are ready to move toward more independent learning. Her goal is that all students will eventually accomplish an independent study by the close of the school year. Mrs. Flarida talks about it this way: "I am constantly on a search—I believe that learning, content, and skills are on a continuum from simple to complex. My responsibility is to determine where a child is currently functioning and to nudge [him or her] onward. I evaluate and make decisions on a constant basis, sometimes informally and sometimes formally. Children who aren't quite ready to be independent learners have an opportunity to gain those skills and then to move on. Children who are ready to be independent learners are encouraged to do so."

Mrs. Flarida would be the first to confirm that teachers using portfolio assessment use a wide variety of interdisciplinary content and instructional approaches to create a dynamic environment that maximizes each student's opportunity to learn and to demonstrate his or her skills and abilities. This dynamic environment means that teachers must utilize a systematic management system to record information, make decisions, and evaluate the impact of those decisions.

Student-Led Conferences

The portfolio assessment process is designed to encourage students to take an active role in their learning and development. Teachers view this role from a number of different dimensions. Some teachers encourage students to keep their own working portfolio, to actively participate in the selection of products/examples of their work, and to self-assess progress. Other teachers are not as comfortable with these activities and limit student access through the use of working portfolios for students and a teacher portfolio (on each student) that may hold confidential data (e.g., standardized tests, parent surveys). Whichever method you choose should fit your school, your classroom, and your teaching philosophy.

One key element in developing student ownership and responsibility is working toward student/teacher conferences. Student/teacher conferences should be designed carefully, particularly at the first attempt. As stated earlier, begin small. Do not expect to have your first student/teacher conference on the entire report card; rather, select an area of study (e.g., writing, a study of oceanography, ect.). Begin by structuring the conference—discuss with the students the format, the questions to ask, and the questions to answer. One of our colleagues structured the student-led conference shown in Figure 4–3.

Try to accomplish two things in your first student/teacher conference: Ask genuine questions and listen carefully. Genishi (1992) has identified those two factors as being critical to the overall success of student-led conferences.

INSIDE A SIXTH-GRADE CLASSROOM

In Kathy Montague's classroom, students are asked to conduct at least one student-led conference. Looking in on the conference from the student's perspective, Figure 4–4 is how it began.

As you can see, Ms. Montague has designed the student-led conference to reflect several elements embedded in the classroom. First, the student can articulate clearly the purpose of the conference ("here to talk about my behavior, participation and learning in class"). The conference also focuses on specific content areas (reading, mathematics, writing, and social studies). Each student provides a written script for the conference and highlights both the strengths and areas needing improvement. Furthermore, each student draws on specific

CONFERENCE # 2
STUDENT'S NOTES

Welcome everyone to the conference. Say something about *why* we are all here today.

To talk about my behavior, participation, and learning in class

READING
First I would like to discuss my strengths, and areas for improvement in reading.
These are the things I think I am really good at in reading.

I'm good at nightly reading and very consistant. I read atleast twice as much as I'm supposed to a night.

Here's why I think I am good at these things (show your proof).

I will show my reading chart

I think I need to spend more time on

writing more words on my vocab sheet so I will expand my vocabulary sheet.

because (show your proof) *You will see the words on my vocab sheet in my writing and on my work.*

Now I would like to demonstrate some of my reading skills for you by playing a tape of myself reading. I chose this piece because

Now is also a good time to discuss how I'm doing on my reading goals for this quarter.
As you remember my goals were to *read at least half an hour. Also spelling and punctuation.*

I think I have done a *good* job because *I read half an hour or an hour every night*

FIGURE 4–3 *Student Conference Planning Notes: Sixth Grade*

WRITING

First I would like to discuss my strengths, and areas for improvement in writing.
These are the things I think I am really good at in writing.

I think I am good at telling details in my pieces and having correct spelling

Here's why I think I am good at these things (show your proof).

I'll show one of my pieces.

I think I need to spend more time on

having better topic sentences that state what the paragraph will be about.

because (show your proof) I will show you the topic sentences in my most recent piece.

Now is also a good time to discuss how I'm doing on my writing goals for this quarter.
As you remember my goals were to Right now in writing we are doing poetry so I cannot prove my goals for writing until poetry is over Things we have learned in poetry is

I think I have done a _____ job because _____

onomatopoeia, metaphors, similes, alliteration, Personification, Haiku We will be having a coffeehouse show so we can share our poetry and all the stuff we learned.

MATH

Here are my math grades. From these grades you can see that I'm doing pretty good at

72% and 61%. I dont think I'm doing very good in math and

and that I could use some work on I don't really understand how to turn decimals into whatever I get confused which is which

(continued)

FIGURE 4–3 *(Continued)*

Now is also a good time to discuss how I'm doing on my math goals for this quarter. As you remember, my goals were to _have a better under-standing of our curriculum._

I think I have done a _____ job because _I will show you that by trying to get atleast 5 Friday Fun sheets with 80% or above._

SOCIAL STUDIES

These are my social studies grades. I'm doing well on _my project on Europe with Melanie. We are very organized and have had a headstart_ and I need to work harder on _not being goofy with Mel when we work on the project even though we still get stuff done._

SCIENCE

The last area I would like to discuss is science. From my grades you can see that I'm doing pretty well on _Rocks + Minerals and on finishing the Jason Project_

and that I could use some work on _working a little faster when we do an assignment._

BEHAVIOR

I know how much behavior can effect my learning, so I would like to tell you a little bit about how I act in school. Generally I _am pretty good and I have lessened my talking in class. Raising my hand more often to answer a question._

I think my behavior has a _big_ effect on my education because _like if you're not listening or goofing around you won't hear or learn._

Do you have any comments, Ms. Montague?

Do you have any comments, Mom and Dad?

Thank your parents for coming. (If you can, think up something _creative_ to end your conference.)

FIGURE 4–3 *(Continued)*

GOAL-SETTING NOTES

Name _Beth_

Date _3rd quarter_

These are my reading goals for this quarter _To write down_
on my vocabulary sheet more
words, and to expand my
vocabulary

These are the things I will show you to prove that I have been working on, or have
achieved my goal(s) _You will see the words_
on my vocabulary sheet,
in my writing and on my
work.

These are my writing goals for this quarter _To work on_
having better topic sentences that
state what the paragraph
will be about

These are the things I will show you to prove that I have been working on, or have
achieved my goal(s) _I will show you the_
topic sentences in my piece.

These are my math goals for this quarter _Have a better_
understanding of our ciricullum

These are the things I will show you to prove that I have been working on, or have
achieved my goal(s) _I will show you that_
by trying to get 5 Friday Fun
Sheets with 80% or above.

I have read, understand, and agree to help my child achieve his/her goals for
this quarter.

Signed _____

Date _____

FIGURE 4–3 *(Continued)*

Confrences
   Welcome to my confrence. mommy this is Kathy Montague. Ms. Montague this is my mom Patty. And this is my dad Mike. We are here to talk about my behavior, participation and learning in class.
   <u>Reading</u>
First we're going to talk about reading, my strengths and areas for improvment. I think I'm good at nightly reading and very consistant. I read atleast twice as much as I'm supposed to every night. Here is my January reading chart. As you can see how much reading I have done I think I need to spend more time on writing down more on my vocab sheet so I will expand my vocabulary. I won't be able to prove this goal because poetry is taking up both writing and reading.
   <u>Writing</u>
   I think I am good at telling details in my pieces and having correct spelling. I can prove those goals by

FIGURE 4–4 *Student Conference Script: Sixth Grade*

showing this piece.

I think I need to spend more time on having better Topic sentences that state what the paragraph will be about.

Also because of the poetry unit we are doing now, I could not acheive this goal. Things we have learned in poetry are is onomatopoeia, metaphore, similes, alliteration, personification, haiku, (hiku). We will be having a coffeehouse on one of the upcoming Fridays to show and share our poetry and what we have learned.

Spelling

My spelling grade is 100% 81% 76%. I don't think I've done that well exept for the 100.

Math

my math grades are 72%, 61%, 76%. I don't think I'm doing very good in math so far I don't fully understand how to measure with a protractor yet but I know how to make an angle with it.

My math goal is to have a better understanding in our math curriculum. I will show that

(continued)

FIGURE 4–4 *(Continued)*

by trying to get 80% or above on atleast 4 Friday Fun Sheets.

<u>Social Studies</u>

My social studies grades are B+, A, 91% or an (A-). I thought I did very well on my Lithuania report last quarter I got a A-. Right now as you know we are studying Europe, Mel and I are doing a report on England. I need to work harder on not being goofy when I work with Mel on our report, even though we still get stuff done.

I think my behavior has a big effect on my education because if you're not listening or goofing around you won't hear or learn.

Do you have any comments, Ms. Montague?

Do you have any questions or comments, mommy or daddy

Thank you for coming?!

FIGURE 4–4 *(Continued)*

evidence from within the portfolio to provide examples at the conference. Finally, it becomes apparent from reading the conference scripts that students have become self-evaluators, jointly responsible for their learning progress with Ms. Montague. For example, throughout the scripts, students noted the following:

> "I think I need to spend more time on having better topic sentences that state what the paragraph will be about."

> "Also because of the poetry unit we are doing now, I could not achieve this goal."

> "My spelling has improved this quarter through my spelling tests and writing tasks."

> "I need to spend more time on my literature log and on the question for the board each week. I need to spend more time on thinking and on writing."

The student-led conference can provide a vital link to the parent/community in understanding student progress and also in providing support for the use of portfolio assessment. In a recent study of parent responses to the use of portfolio during conferences, parents overwhelmingly indicated a greater degree of satisfaction with conferences using portfolios of student work (Shaklee et al., 1990). As one parent noted, "I now have real information to discuss. I can see how to help my child; I know what they are doing. It's so much easier than trying to understand a letter grade." Furthermore, teachers also reported a greater degree of satisfaction, fewer problem conferences, and greater responsiveness on the part of participants (e.g., family members, parents, and/or guardians). In addition to the student/teacher conferences led by the student, portfolios can provide information to differentiate instruction at the individual level.

INDIVIDUALIZED PLANNING AND PORTFOLIOS

In looking at a few of the ways in which portfolio evidence can be used, examples have ranged from the global (e.g., use of questioning strategies) to the more specific (e.g., student-led conferences). Next is an example that looks very specifically at the development of one student—how the teacher makes decisions and how those decisions are reflected in the portfolio evidence.

As you will recall, Mary Anne Davis teaches in a second-grade classroom. She has created a portfolio assessment system for her students in mathematics based on the local curriculum course of study, the state requirements, and the information provided by the National Council of Teachers of Mathematics. As part of the process, each of her students has a mathematics portfolio. Students use the portfolio to examine their understanding of a particular concept as well as to provide peer review for other students.

In addition, as Mary Anne reads each student portfolio, she provides comments, corrections, and clarification of particular elements. In looking through several samples of Janie's work (Figure 4–5), you will begin to under-

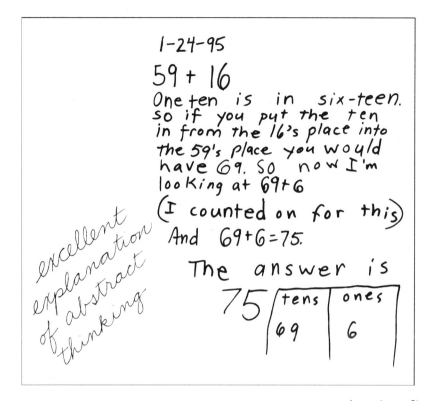

1-24-95

59 + 16

One ten is in six-teen.
so if you put the ten
in from the 16's place into
the 59's place you would
have 69. So now I'm
looking at 69+6

(I counted on for this)

And 69+6=75.

The answer is

75

tens	ones
69	6

excellent explanation of abstract thinking

(continued)

FIGURE 4–5   *Teacher Response to Math Portfolio*

I Have _____.

Everyone gets a card.
anybody can go 1st. Jay you're
first. read your card.

• I have 50.
who has
10 more?

whoever has how many more or
that numbe less they
read they're card.

• I have 60.
who has
11 less?

Excellent!
explanation
Good grasp of
place value
d regrouping!

and it keeps going on

• I have 49.
Who has
49 less?

you can
stop whenever
you want.

• I have 0.
who has
22 more?

• I nave
22. who
has 40
more?

FIGURE 4–5 *(Continued)*

GREAT JOB because you won.

$$57$$
$$+26$$
$$83$$

I'm _so_ proud of you
You were the only one
who got it right.

YIPPIE. From
            Janie
2-10-95

Dear Mary.
I'm sorry you didn't get /
right. the correct answer
is 83. not 713.

$$57$$
$$+26$$
$$83$$

This is what I woud've
done if I were you.
Find out what 7+6=
13. Put the 3 on the
bottom 1 on top
1+5+2=8

$$\begin{array}{r} 5\,7 \\ 2\,6 \\ \hline \end{array}$$

$$\begin{array}{r} {}^{1}5\,7 \\ 2\,6 \\ \hline 3 \end{array}$$

$$\begin{array}{r} 5\,7 \\ 2\,6 \\ \hline 8\ 3 \end{array}$$

83. From Janie 2-10-95

Dear Bill. I'm sorry but you
probably thought 1+5+2=7. But
it's 8.
        You just got mixed up.
Next time check your
answer. Regroup it. because
7+6=13 3 goes on the bottom.
1 goes on top of 5. for 57.
        Bye,
            From Janie 2-10-95

FIGURE 4–5 *(Continued)*

stand Janie as a mathematician and Mary Anne's role as facilitator/teacher.

IN CLOSING

The purpose of portfolio assessment is to collect information/evidence of student growth, over time, and to use this evidence to make better decisions on behalf of students. Coupled with the teacher's role is the role of students in the learning process—engaging students in active learning and helping students to accept responsibility for their learning. This chapter was designed to give you a variety of ways to think about using the portfolio assessment information to better inform your teaching.

AT A GLANCE...
Moving from Assessment to Instruction

◆ Portfolio information should directly reflect the goals of the classroom.

◆ Portfolio information should be used to make effective decisions on behalf of students.

◆ There are a variety of ways to differentiate curriculum and instructional strategies to provide a "better match" for students.

◆ Begin slowly to use portfolio information to make decisions; evaluate the effect of those decisions on students as well as on yourself.

Chapter 5

Shifting Assessment Paradigms

2-26-97

Parent conferences—always a stressful time. Trying to get a comprehensive report of each child's progress done in less than a half hour and still trying to discuss parent concerns is always an impossible task. I tried to go over the portfolios as they are—in progress—to see if there was any way I could use them for the conferences. Well, since we have fleshed out the rubric for writing, the criteria for evaluating progress seems so clear that I decided to share it with a few of the parents before showing them the writing samples in the portfolio. The parents seemed to understand exactly how their child's work fit with the rubric. It seemed so concrete—I wonder if I could include the kids in these conferences next time.

3-24-97

The portfolio work is taking less time since I've let the kids be responsible for filing and managing the collection of info. I think I can live with the change—especially since my district has been so supportive with in-services and Sally's availability. I would just love to have the time to sit down with the other teachers and find out how they are making it work. I wonder if I asked, would they let us do that? I need time to think about what it is that I am doing differently....

The process of instituting change—whether it be at the classroom level, the district level, or the national level—is never an easy one. There are logistical considerations as well as attitudinal barriers facing teachers as they try to shift their paradigms. This final chapter will examine the issues involved in making changes in assessment practices.

DEVELOPING PERSPECTIVE

Teachers are concerned with enabling children to have the opportunity to learn and flourish within school settings. By using portfolios, children's learning can be represented in meaningful, systematic ways. If teachers genuinely believe they are responsible for making the best of schools, they need to consider curriculum, teaching strategies, and assessment procedures that are in the best interests of children. Portfolio assessment, using multiple sources for assessing children's learning, is one of the ways to improve the educational process for all children.

Assuming that the concept of portfolios is new to most teachers, the development and understanding of portfolio use becomes something that is experienced individually and collectively with colleagues through supported, deliberative actions. School district staff-development efforts often are the vehicle to sustain teachers' quests for continued professional knowledge. However, proposed innovation of teaching practice is often attempted through staff development that rarely focuses on teacher perceptions of classroom environments, practices, or students (Fullan, 1993).

Staff development for teachers is often incongruous with teachers' perceived needs for professional growth. As you consider the recommendations for staff development to facilitate this paradigm shift, also consider the multiple layers and levels of teachers' experiences and interactions. Where do you begin to effect change?

CHANGE AT THE MICROLEVEL

Sometimes the desire to change practice first occurs at the individual classroom level, as was the case with Mary Anne Davis. A teacher may feel the need to use different strategies for assessing his or her students because the old ways do not meet current needs. There are both benefits and barriers to making this individual shift. The benefits are that you do not need to wait for colleagues or the system to see the need for change. You can merely develop a personal plan for action and proceed. The drawbacks are that you have no precedents or models to follow. Also, you may end up with changes that are incompatible with grade report expectations. Finally, there may be no time carved out for you to experiment with innovations.

Mary Anne, an experienced teacher, was equipped to handle the risk for potential failure of the innovation. She was able to solicit help and understanding from the parents. She did not abandon her traditional methods of assessment in the transition. She took her time to reflect on the process.

CHANGE AT THE MACROLEVEL

Sometimes change comes about from above, not necessarily from a "celestial" level. Rather, school-, district-, or state-level administrators determine the time for change. One of the benefits in these instances is that there is likely to be technical assistance available to you as you learn to do portfolio assessment. Another benefit is that there is potential collegial support for working through the changes. The drawbacks include a potential lack of personal input regarding timing, process, and strategies.

Mrs. Bain's journal account is a good example of top-down change. She experienced resentment about forced change, she was placed in a position of doubting her own understanding of the process, and she worried about whether she was doing the best she could for her students. On the other hand, Mrs. Bain had a curriculum director who was sensitive to the need to provide technical support in the form of in-service and consultation. The coordinator made the shift from traditional report cards to portfolios so that the teachers did not have to lobby for time conservation. Finally, the plan for change was gradual, allowing for teacher perspectives to "catch up" to innovations.

THE REALITIES OF SHIFTING PARADIGMS

Whether change occurs from the bottom up or the top down, there are a number of variables to be considered. We will state them first quite simply and then elaborate on how each variable can be addressed at micro- and macrolevel shifts. The variables include consideration of time, support/technical assistance, transition from traditional to innovative assessment, accountability, and reflectivity.

As change in schools is considered, one must also look at the realities of teachers' lives in schools. Teachers talk to each other about personal and professional issues. Teachers discuss with each other about what they are doing in their classrooms. Teachers observe how their colleagues do things and reflect on both the congruence and differences in practice. Teachers can feel isolated in classrooms unless opportunities for collaboration are available. Teachers have a wide range of professional experience and personal experience. All of these realities

---

AT A GLANCE...
Realities of Shifting Paradigms

◆ Teachers must be given opportunities to develop new perspectives.

◆ Change occurs at both the micro- and macro-levels.

◆ There are variables that must be considered:
- Time
- Support/Technical Assistance
- Transition from Traditional to Innovative Assessment
- Accountability
- Reflectivity

suggest that change may be different for each individual involved, yet the potential for collegial support is there.

Time

If there were a way to bottle and sell it, time would make someone a fortune. In almost any setting where change is occurring, time is the one commodity of which there is never enough. The shift to portfolio assessment from traditional forms of assessment, at first, appears to require more time. Yet, as we interviewed teachers who had been given some time to make the shift, they reported that the time required for this form of assessment had not really added to their burden. In fact, many teachers reported that the time it took to provide more exciting, student-centered curriculum decreased because more individuals were involved in contributing data to the assessment process. As one teacher put it, "At first, I thought 'How will I ever manage all of it?'... and, at first, it did take more time. But once you get into the routine and figure out how to involve the children,... I don't think I spend more time on it [portfolio assessment] than I had."

Microlevel Time Management Beth Trivelli and Amy Adams were two of the teachers involved in the Early Assessment of Exceptional Potential Project. As members of the pilot and subsequent project, they were in on the grass-roots planning for the portfolio assessment process. They were committed to trying the shift and making it work. But they were also aware of the extra time the process seemed to take when placed alongside all of their other classroom responsibilities. They became aware of their need to confer with other colleagues in the project, so they approached their building principal to see if they could have a common planning time. The principle agreed to this, and these teachers instantly had a pocket of time in which to collaborate on the implementation of the portfolio assessment process. The added time was an easy resource to secure for these teachers.

Kathy Montague had already committed herself to portfolio assessment when she began to problem solve how she could report such rich assessment data to parents. She decided to institute parent/teacher/student conferences to accomplish this goal. She developed her system for three-way conferences in order to place the student in the role of responsible participant. In this way, she managed to communicate a wealth of information to the family in a short period of time. Her time was conserved by relinquishing some of the control ordinarily held by the teacher alone. These days, Kathy's time is better spent, she says, in facilitating the student role. Consequently, time previously spent on paperwork is now spent on teaching life skills.

Macrolevel Time Management In one school district, the decision was made to move to portfolio assessment over a time period of several years. The administration mapped out how this would occur and developed a timeline for activities to occur in order to meet this goal. Clearly, there was an administrative expression of respect for the amount of time it takes to shift long-held paradigms.

The first year was a planning year in which a small group of people determined what information was needed to institute change. The most important piece of information needed was a statement of guidelines for pupil performance. A faculty group took the state guidelines and developed a set of goals/objectives for each grade level that were intended as a framework for the portfolio assessment process. Once this was completed, the second year was used as a planning time for the teachers to learn how to develop a portfolio assessment based on the grade-level objectives. One content area was developed at a time. The shift to the portfolio assessment process was to take place over a two-year period.

In another part of the country, several districts that were moving toward more authentic forms of assessment hired a consultant whose salary was shared by the districts. This person's job was to assist each district with its particular assessment needs. Although the task of juggling all districts' concerns without really having a home base was difficult for the consultant, he was able to do the needed work that could not otherwise have been completed by individual districts. It was, in essence, a macrolevel time management solution.

Support/Technical Assistance

Perhaps there are some individuals who are most comfortable operating in a renegade mode, but most people prefer to have some sort of a support system in place as they make changes. Simply stated, teachers need (and want) to talk to other teachers about their practices, their assumptions, and their beliefs about how learning occurs and how it can be measured. Collaboration seems to promote more points of view, more problem solving, and more energy. Yet, the plan for change does not necessarily include a plan for support. And plans for support often involve the need for technical assistance.

Microlevel Support/Technical Assistance   Amy Adams and Beth Trivelli are two teachers who exemplify the benefits of support and technical assistance. In the midst of their shift to portfolio assessment as part of the EAEP, their school became a Schools of the Future site. This was an added bonus, as it gave license for flexibility and innovation. As the teachers in the primary grades worked in their common planning times, they began to experience conflict among themselves. Change, by its very nature, induces a need to contrast and compare ideas, both old and new. In a group of ordinarily collegial people, negative feelings were beginning to interfere with their transition. They requested and received support in learning how to resolve conflict successfully. The results of these efforts were positive in moving them all ahead with change.

A less supportive story comes from Lisa Biclawski, a teacher whose district was not involved in the EAEP. Lisa told us that although her district developed a report card, her building administrator was encouraging the teachers to use authentic forms of assessment (such as portfolios) in conjunction with the report card. Consequently, she is required to use report cards but has instituted portfolio assessment as well. There has been no guidance given from the administration for how, when, and in what form the portfolio assessment should be done. Consequently, Lisa has been seeking the "right" way to approach portfolio assessment. She has formed informal alliances with teachers who are trying to learn the process, she has attended all professional development sessions that she can find, and she has enrolled in an individual investigation at the university with a professor who promotes portfolio assessment. All of her efforts are informal in nature, spurred by the encouragement from her building administrator.

Lisa is motivated by the results she sees: "Portfolios represent growth.... You can look at a portfolio at the end of the year and see the growth.... Kids take ownership of the portfolio." Lisa has used the portfolio to plan instruction, to modify curriculum, and as an integral part of her parent conferences. She feels that report cards will soon be a thing of the past, though parents still seem to want the concrete feedback that grades offer.

Lisa's story suggests that the support and technical assistance on the local level may not be readily available. On the other hand, her story suggests that change can be supported in an informal way by finding colleagues who are also shifting assessment paradigms. She shared that the teachers who are part of her support system often disagree on methods but are willing to listen and provide suggestions. They are all committed to the process because of their personal successes and in spite of the lack of more global forms of support.

Macrolevel Support / Technical Assistance The EAEP included clear plans for the macrolevel support and technical assistance required for shifts in practice. The first year of the grant, we provided in-service training to the teachers who were piloting the portfolio assessment process. The two-hour training sessions involved an introduction to the actual instruments they would use and an explanation of how and when to complete them. We discovered quite quickly that it takes much more than a two-hour in-service training session in order for teachers to implement an innovative process. We learned much from this experience about how and when teachers need support and technical assistance. The teachers provided excellent critiques to guide our planning for the next phases of the project.

One of the outgrowths of our pilot work was a two-week summer institute for teachers in which they learned about the early assessment of exceptional potential and the portfolio assessment process. The institute was carefully planned to include presentations about exceptional potential/giftedness, the complexity of identifying underrepresented populations (minority and economically disadvantaged groups), and curriculum strategies that allow for observing exceptional potential. We also included a very focused component to assist teachers in developing their observational skills and, specifically, their ability to "see" identifiers of exceptional potential. The need to provide hands-on practical training was clear from the pilot experience.

A second outgrowth of our pilot experience was the plan for district-specific support that was created by the teachers at the end of the summer institute. The project offered support in the form of graduate assistants who worked in the classrooms on a regular basis, faculty who were available for consultation, and regular meetings with the project team during the year to review work in progress and assist in the final portfolio evaluations.

The district support plans varied from one district to the next (see Figure 5–1). Although the actual implementations occurred on a more microlevel, the plans were constructed on a macrolevel. In some cases, the support consisted of data collection (e.g., observations of lessons, administration of surveys) or in the form of lesson demonstrations, or teaching lessons so that teachers could observe. In other cases, the support team helped design and implement curriculum interventions based on action plans for target students. The results of the district-specific plans were quite positive. It was evident to all of us involved that change at this magnitude must have a scaffold of support and technical assistance undergirding it. When such structures are in place, teachers are willing to take the risks that change entails.

Several of us have had the opportunity to consult with other districts who have used the EAEP model. In each district, support and technical assistance has been an important part of the plan. In one case, one of the EAEP investigators was contracted to provide in-service training for two days at the beginning of the grant, send the teachers on their way to institute the portfolio assessments, and then return to assist in the evaluation of the portfolios. The coordinator of gifted education was the

SUPPORT TEAM

BUILDING/DISTRICT

WHAT	WHEN	WHO (person/resource)
Send home parent communication as part of orientation and/or Open House	Early Sept. 1996	Total Team: Cycle I and II • Prior to school starting, Lois will provide letters and form • Lois will talk to Bev for permission • Judy will talk to other teachers
Cycle I and II Staff Meeting • Answer questions – Cycle II teachers • Compile data from Parent Survey	Sept. 23, 1996, 3:45 Bissell	Lois will call meeting
Tape lesson	Before Sept. 23, 1996	Greg – Roseanna
Review tape		Cycle I and II
Plan for team teaching time		Total Team

FIGURE 5–1 *EAEP District Support Plan*

technical assistant in the interim. Success was moderate in the adoption of the portfolio process. In this case, more technical assistance may have increased the success.

In other replications of the EAEP model, other plans for support and technical assistance have occurred. In each instance, the replications have varied in terms of commitment to support for change. Overall, it seems clear that there is a major need for a well-defined plan prior to instituting change.

Transition from Traditional to Innovative Assessment

Innovation implies new practice. Since some form of assessment has been occurring prior to the institution of alternative forms of assessment, then something must be given up. In the case of portfolio assessment, we hear of teachers, schools, districts, and beyond who move to portfolio assessment and then wonder what they can do about report cards. It seems that it takes that experience of juxtaposing a rich, qualitative assessment (a portfolio) against a thinner quantitative assessment (a report card) before people are willing to let go of the "known." In the case of Lisa, she believes that the parents are the stumbling block because they want the concrete, normative symbols of grades in order to understand how their children are doing in school. She predicts that as the district committee begins its periodic review of the report card format, it will shift to portfolios instead of report cards.

In all of these cases, it has taken some logistical strategizing in order to accomplish the shift. Yet, the shift must occur at both the micro- and macrolevels for the change to take hold.

Microlevel Transition from Traditional to Innovative Assessment The kindergarten teachers in a local school were exploring their practices in light of NAEYC's statement regarding developmentally appropriate practices. They observed each other's classrooms. They redesigned their rooms. They developed curriculum that emerged from the children's interests and integrated the content areas. They collected wonderful data indicating their children's progress. And, they felt utterly stifled when they were forced to reduce all of these "best practices" to a report card format. The group of five stood up in protest to their principal and demanded an end to report cards. Though it sounds like a dramatic insurrection, the shift to portfolio assessment occurred in a deliberate and orderly way over the course of three months. The teachers took ownership for creating the shift to innovative practice.

Macrolevel Transition from Traditional to Innovative Assessment The shift at the district level is not always a smooth one. In some districts where portfolios have been instituted, parents have demanded the "known" forms of accountability (i.e., report cards) rather than learn about portfolio data. It is essential that communication about such changes be clearly communicated to parents. In fact, parents should be integral members of planning committees working toward innovative shifts. They are important partners in the move to alternative assessment.

Other macrolevel issues involve some districtwide communication of standards for evaluating portfolios. In one district, a committee has been formed to develop a district assessment system. The committee consists of elementary and secondary faculty, special education faculty, community members, and university/college specialists as resources. The assessment system has three components.

The first component consists of informed teacher judgment or bodies of evidence collected by teachers, such as essays, response tests, teacher observations, and personal communications. Frameworks for evaluating the evidence include the most appropriate assessment strategies, timelines for assessment, how multiple points of view will be included and aggregated, and samples of actual assessments.

The second component is student validation. Students, with the assistance of teachers and parents, build a portfolio of data demonstrating attainment of content standards. The collection process is also an instructional tool to help students navigate their way toward meeting/ exceeding the standards.

The third component is the districtwide assessment. This would occur at level transitions and include selected response tests and norm-referenced tests, as well as focus on particular standards. District results are reported in terms of percentages of students meeting standards.

This district assessment system is an example of how a top-down process has been carefully constructed to include the best elements of portfolio assessment practices, multiple levels of ownership, and a feasible plan for implementation. The inclusion of teachers in the development and institutionalization should ensure success to this plan for innovation.

Accountability

The future of the world is dependent on the next generation being able to assume control responsibly. When the popular press looks at society's ills, blame is often laid at the feet of schools. Though this seems like a rather simplistic and reductionistic way of approaching society's problems, it clearly indicates that educational institutions are indeed accountable to society. Perhaps this explains why schools are so slow to shift paradigms. In fact, many of those opposed to a shift in assessment practices worry about the potential of portfolio assessment to produce accountability data. Essentially, there is the dilemma of the value of quantitative versus qualitative evidence. As one considers the kinds of accountability issues involved, resolutions can be seen at both the micro- and macrolevels.

Microlevel Accountability Teachers at the classroom level have a number of different constituents to whom they are responsible. First, they are responsible to the students to provide feedback about how they are progressing. Second, they are responsible to parents to convey an accurate and timely assessment of their child's progress. Finally, they are responsible to the school to report group progress, appropriateness of curriculum guidelines, and "match" of students to program. This, in essence, defines the microlevel chain of accountability.

Kathy Montague's story offers a look at how one can be responsive to both students and parents. Kathy engaged in portfolio assessment because she was convinced that it would provide more meaningful feedback to her, to students, and to parents. She found, quite quickly, that the students gained a more accurate perception of their progress and that they seemed to develop ownership of their progress. By establishing a portfolio data-collection process, Kathy provided students with an avenue for being accountable to themselves. In each case, the students were guided by her in the role of self-evaluation and self-direction. When unrealistic plans were developed, Kathy assisted the students in understanding how and why revisions needed to occur. In a way, Kathy's plan addresses an area in which many adults are lacking skills.

Kathy also defined accountability in relation to the parents of her students. The traditional forms of assessment (i.e., report cards) did not, in her opinion, account for the important skills and attitudes she saw her students developing in her approach to portfolio assessment and conferencing process. She developed a system of communicating with parents on a regular basis through phone calls, conferences, and materials that were sent home for responses. The triadic process that Kathy developed (child, parent, teacher) placed all parties in a position of hearing, responding, and planning together. By creating the collaborative interactions, Kathy short-circuited the potential for misunderstanding as much as possible. She also encouraged parents and children to communicate their views on progress and plans for future work.

Mary Anne sent a letter home to her students' parents to inform them about the shift to portfolio assessment. In this way, she made sure that she was accountable for changes that they were about to see in her assessment process. She accomplished an important goal in any innovation—eliciting the support of constituents.

Macrolevel Accountability The shift to portfolio assessment is, in essence, a shift from quantitative to qualitative reporting. For the sake of manageability, quantitative data are far easier to handle, interpret, and archive. This is the system that schools have depended on for years. Consequently, with the move to portfolio assessment, there needs to be a concurrent shift in how qualitative data are managed. The movement toward outcome-based assessment in many communities may hold promise for a fit with portfolio assessment. For instance, one district created a checklist system for expected outcomes and required documentation of each outcome be provided in a portfolio. Time will tell whether this sort of solution satisfies the need for accountability on a macrolevel.

Reflectivity

The nature of portfolio assessment requires participants who are reflective practitioners. Reflective practitioners are those individuals who can transcend their own personal teaching experiences and view their teaching (and all this involves) from multiple perspectives and through the current knowledge derived from theory and research (Clandinin, 1985). The reflective practitioner values the integration of theory and practice and thinking about one's own teaching. Certainly, the process of implementing portfolio assessment is reflective, not mechanical. Yet, some of the potential barriers to this shift in practice preclude reflectivity. Most notably, it takes time to be reflective. It is a cerebral, analytical activity. It also takes a particular disposition to be reflective. This disposition is one that is not built into the traditional reward systems under which teachers operate.

Reflectivity at the Microlevel In almost every example of teachers making the move to portfolio assessment, there were instances where the teachers reviewed and revised their plans. In the case of Jenny Cos, she planned a particular strategy for collecting data and found, upon reflection, that she was not gathering enough information to help her plan curriculum and instruction. She revisited her plan and decided that she wanted more regular feedback and conferencing with parents along the way. As a kindergarten teacher, this better suited her needs.

Lisa Biclawski has been implementing her portfolio assessment process as she thinks about what she wants and confers with other teachers. She observes how others have gathered data and thinks about how productive her efforts have been. As she does this, she modifies and improves her plan.

Kathy Montague's experiences demonstrate a long-term process of reflectivity, revision, and revisiting. She slowly developed rubrics, methods for recording process, and evaluation of the data over time. Rather than viewing each change as discrete, Kathy sees her long-term efforts as an evolution of her teaching style. None of this was possible without serious reflection.

Reflectivity at the Macrolevel The primary issue at the macrolevel has to do with how to encourage educators to become reflective. At the preservice teacher education level, the question of how to prepare future teachers to be reflective is a difficult one. Are there courses, exercises, or experiences that assist in developing this ability? Is there a particular disposition that one has for being reflective? Is it possible to be a "good" teacher without being reflective? These are questions that seem to guide inquiry about reflectivity.

IN CLOSING

A number of issues have been identified that seem to provide potential barriers to those interested in shifting assessment paradigms. These issues have to do with time, support/technical assistance, transition from traditional to innovative assessment, accountability, and reflectivity. Examples have been provided that show successful negotiation of these issues at both the micro- and macrolevels. We believe that these issues are not insurmountable but challenges that have rewarding payoffs. In fact, the path to portfolio assessment is a clear one as far as can be seen.

Epilogue

5-20-97

Well, here it is, almost the end of the school year. I peeked back at the beginning of my journal and was surprised at how far I have shifted in my thinking about assessment. I had no idea last summer what was in store for me. Part of me is excited about how flexible my ideas about teaching have become over the last year. Another part of me wonders whether I've done the right thing by discarding some of those old practices. Did I learn as much about the kids this year? Did I let anyone slip through the cracks? Did I plan differently? Did every kid do his or her best? I need time this summer to just sit back and think about these changes—think about how I would do it differently, better. It seems that I got closer to the kids and families this year... my kids were able to be more independent. For now, I'll save the questions for some clear thinking time.

If you finished this book with more questions and ideas than you did narrow answers, then it has done the task we intended. Portfolio assessment, like all good teaching practices, has some parameters that strengthen the design, support interaction between and among stakeholders, and provide a rich, in-depth portrait of a student's learning.

Portfolio assessment also has some unique aspects that can only be the decision of the teacher or team that uses it. Decisions noted in Chapter 2 such as "What are the criteria, how long should we collect, or how do we make decisions?" inform the process and create a framework for the design. By using both a broad view and a local view of a dynamic curriculum-assessment-instruction model, you will strengthen your views, enhance the likelihood of accurate decisions, and maintain a reasonable standard by which student learning can be assessed.

As in many situations, your views of learning, curriculum, assessment, and instructional practice are critical to the development and implementation of a sound portfolio assessment system. "Clearing the lenses" by which you view growth and development, assuring that you acknowledge and examine your biases, as well as constructing learning environments that allow students to "show what they know" are all crucial to effective assessment.

Further, as one reconsiders the relationship between home and school, it is easy to see the important part that parents, guardians, family, and community members must have in education. Portfolio assessment models make explicit your commitment to genuine dialogue, support, and joint decision making. In such systems, not only is the *responsibility* shared but so is the *power*.

We know that the design and implementation of a sound portfolio assessment system takes *time*—time to learn, time to practice, and time to implement. Educators never feel as if they have enough time; however, if you are going to broaden the basis by which you assess performance and achievement, then you must take the time to do it to the best of your ability.

Finally, students, family members, parents, and, most importantly, teachers have acknowledged the importance and worthiness of portfolio assessment models. Although not without problems, with one voice, they note, "This is the most worthwhile educational innovation I have done in a long time. After twenty-seven years in the classroom, I have finally learned how to use my observations and notes to make better decisions for my students. What else could be more important?"

Bibliography

Bersani, C., & Barbour, N. (1991). *Ohio early childhood curriculum guide*. Ohio Department of Education.

Beyer, B. (1991). What philosophy offers to the teaching of thinking. In A. Costa (Ed.), *Developing minds: A resource book for teaching thinking* (pp. 72–76). Washington, DC: Association for Supervision and Curriculum Development.

Bredekamp, S. (Ed.). (1987). *Developmentally appropriate practice in early childhood programs serving children from birth through age 8*. Washington, DC: National Association for the Education of Young Children.

Bredekamp, S., & Rosegrant, T. (Eds.). (1992). *Reaching potentials: Appropriate curriculum and assessment for young children*. Washington, DC: National Association for the Education of Young Children.

Clandinin, D. J. (1985). Personal practical knowledge: A study of teachers' classroom images. *Curriculum Inquiry, 15,* 361–385.

Costa, A. (Ed). (1991). *Developing minds: A resource book for teaching thinking* (Vol. 1). Washington, DC: Association for Supervision and Curriculum Development.

Davies, A., Cameron, C., Politano, C., & Gregory, K. (1992). *Together is better: Collaborative assessment, evaluation and reporting*. Winnepeg, Canada: Peguis Publishers.

Delisle, J. (1992). *Guiding the social and emotional development of gifted youth*. New York: Longman.

Fullan, M. (1993). Innovation, reform, and restructuring strategies. In G. Cawelti (Ed.), *Challenges and achievements of American education: 1993 Yearbook of the Association for Supervision and Curriculum Development*. Alexandria, VA: ASCD.

Genishi, C. (Ed.). (1992). *Ways of assessing children and curriculum*. New York: Teachers College Press.

Jacobs, H. (Ed.). (1989). *Interdisciplinary curriculum: Design and implementation*. Alexandria, VA: Association for Supervision and Curriculum Development.

Kapinus, B. (1986). *Ready reading readiness*. Baltimore, MD: Maryland State Department of Education.

McAfee, O., & Leong, D. (1994). *Assessing and guiding young children's development and learning*. Boston: Allyn and Bacon.

McTighe, J., & Lyman, F. (1991). Cueing thinking in the classroom: The promise of theory-embedded tools. In A. Costa (Ed.), *Developing minds: A resource book for teaching thinking* (pp. 243–250). Washington, DC: Association for Supervision and Curriculum Development.

National Association of the State Boards of Education (NASBE). (1988). *Right from the start: The report of the NASBE Task Force on Early Childhood Education*. Alexandria, VA: NASBE.

O'Brien, L. M. (1993). Teacher values and classroom culture: Teaching and learning in a rural Appalachian Head Start program. *Early Education and Development, 4* (1), 5–19.

Paul, R. (1991). Teaching critical thinking in the strong sense. In A. Costa (Ed.), *Developing minds: A resource book for teaching thinking* (pp. 77–84). Washington, DC: Association for Supervision and Curriculum Development.

Paulson, L., & Paulson, P. (1990). *How do portfolios measure up?* Paper presented at the meeting of the Northwest Evaluation Association, Union, WA.

Perkins, D. N. (1991). What creative thinking is. In A. Costa (Ed.), *Developing minds: A resource book for teaching thinking* (pp. 85–88). Washington, DC: Association for Supervision and Curriculum Development.

Perrone, V. (Ed.). (1991). *Expanding student assessment*. Alexandria, VA: Association for Supervision and Curriculum Development.

Shaklee, B. (1993). Preliminary findings of the Early Assessment for Exceptional Potential Project. *Roeper Review, 16* (2), 105–109.

Shaklee, B., Barbour, N., Whitmore, J., Ambrose, R., & Viechnicki, K. (1990). *Early assessment for exceptional potential in young minority and/or economically disadvantaged students*. Washington, DC: U.S. Department of Education, Office of Educational Research Improvement.

Shaklee, B., & Viechnicki, K. (1995). A qualitative approach to port-folios: The Early Assessment for Exceptional Potential Design. *Journal for the Education of the Gifted, 19* (2), 156–170.

Spodek, B., & Saracho, O. (1994). *Right from the start.* Boston: Allyn and Bacon.

VanTassel-Baska, J. (1994). *Comprehensive curriculum for gifted learners.* Boston: Allyn and Bacon.

Viechnicki, K., Barbour, N., Shaklee, B., Rohrer, J., & Ambrose, R. (1993). The impact of portfolio assessment on teacher classroom activities. *Journal of Teacher Education, 44* (2), 371–377.

Wiggins. G. (1993). *Assessing student performance: Exploring the purpose and limits of testing.* New York: Jossey-Bass.

Wolfgang, C. H., & Wolfgang, M. E. (1992). *School for young children.* Boston: Allyn and Bacon.